BEACH BOYS ARCH

VOLUME 3

FOREWORD

DENNIS WILSON

Although it seeemd like 1976 was the year that the Beach Boys jumped back into the public spotlight - and public acceptance - the truth is somewhat more involved.

Although Capitol had been reissuing Beach Boys albums and creating collections throughout their career, the timing was right with the public when the Endless Summer compilation was released in 1974, and quickly followed up with another, Spirit of America, the same year. The Beach Boys toured with Chicago in 1975, and by 1976, the band that had seen concert attendance fall off in America were once again playing in large stadiums and sold-out crowds.

Brian was (it appeared) back at the helm and 15 Big Ones had enough rock and roll to remind America what they liked about the band most. *Rock and Roll Music* and the follow-up single, *It's OK*, gave the public what they wanted most from their band...good time rock & roll.

This volume offers some items from their first 15 years but focuses mostly on artifacts and materials from 1976 through the present. Because of the copyright laws, what is already in the public domain and what we have permission to republish, there are fewer magazine articles here and more PR materials, promotional advertising and such...still interesting for the true fan.

ISBN 978-1-941028-01-8
Copyright 2014 White Lightning Publications

BRIAN WILSON

It's been
fun, fun, fun

Thank you,
Alan, Brian, Carl, Dennis and Mike
The Beach Boys

The Beach Boys
15 Big Ones

4

DENNIS WILSON

CARL WILSON

BRIAN WILSON

MIKE LOVE

AL JARDINE

Exclusive Interview
THE BEACH BOYS

by Elliot Cohen

The Beach Boys. The mere mention of the name immediately conjures bikini-clad young ladies with smiles that could melt your heart, drive-in movies, blistering sun rays tempered by ice cold cokes, summer night breezes, fast cars and even "faster" cheerleaders shaking their pom-poms at the big high school football game. An idyllic world unencumbered by parental or adult responsibilities.

Over the past 18 years the three Wilson brothers, Brian, Dennis and Carl, cousin Mike Love, and childhood friend Alan Jardine, have all become millionaires propagating a California myth which they helped to create in the sixties though Brian Wilson's masterful compositions.

From a somewhat auspicious recording debut in 1961 with a primative sounding ode to brother Dennis' favorite sport, *Surfin'*, through the merging of the breezy harmonies of The Four Freshmen, the rollicking guitar sounds of Chuck Berry, and the burgeoning talents of Brian Wilson as a composer, arranger, and producer, the Beach Boys went on to become *the* greatest American rock band of them all.

IT hasn't all been smooth sailing for the group though. In the band's heyday from 1963-1966 they could do no wrong, and easily rivaled The Beatles, whose work they frequently eclipsed, particularly in terms of classic hit singles. Then in mid-1966 Brian, who was becoming heavily influenced by the use of LSD, created **Pet Sounds**, one of rock's genuine masterpieces. The most sophisticated work produced in rock till then, the album seemed too bizarre to be palatable. It ended up being the group's first real commercial failure.

Later that year, in the final burst of their original glory, The Beach Boys produced *Good Vibrations,* one of the most innovative singles of all time. *Good Vibrations* briefly established the Beach Boys as *the* most important rock group in the world. However, while working on the next album, which was to be called **Smile,** the eccentric Brian Wilson destroyed the tapes and the Beatles eclipsed both The Beach Boys and the entire rock world with **Sargent Pepper's.** When the Beach Boys finally released their new album, a hastily underproduced effort called **Smiley Smile,** coming nearly 16 months after their previous effort, **Pet Sounds,** their momentum had been lost, and the group's artistic and commercial fortunes nosedived.

However, in 1975, during a four-year period in which the group wasn't recording any new albums, Capitol released an album of their early hits titled **Endless Summer.** This album earned the Beach Boys their first gold album in years, but more important, it brought an entire new generation of fans flocking to their concerts. Although the band has managed only one top ten single in the past 11 years, in concert, the magic is still

The Beach Boys in 1966

Mike Love

Bruce Johnston

there. The members are no longer "boys": all of them are bearded and several are either balding, greying, or paunchy. Yet they still fill stadiums with concert-goers young enough to be their own kids.

ALTHOUGH someone close to the band once commented that the only harmony within the group is vocal, they have still managed to turn a bumpy surf into a sea of tranquility long enough to have spanned the crew-cut era of The Kingston Trio to the spiked hair era of The Sex Pistols. Now they are once again touring to promote their twenty-third studio album, **L.A. Light Album.**

Lead guitarist Carl Wilson is relaxing in his New York hotel suite on a Sunday afternoon accompanied by part-time Beach Boy Bruce Johnston and his wife, their road manager Jerry Shilling, and several people from Epic Records. Up close, the inherent boyishness still peers through from behind the bearded exterior of the 32-year-old Wilson's face, which still has the appearance of a college student who thinks the added facial hair will make him look more mature. The youngest Beach Boy still retains a certain amount of baby fat around the cheeks as well as the rotund torso bulging through his baby-blue jogging suit.

As for the title of the new album, the recently-arisen Beach Boy explains in a still sleepy voice, "I was doing a spiritual exercise one day looking at a candle, which I always have by me when I'm meditating and the words **Beach Boys L.A.** came out of nowhere. Then the words **Light Album** appeared!"

CARL'S voice perks up and his eyes

Al Jardine

Carl Wilson

widen as though he had just stumbled upon the wisdom of the ages. He has lately been converted from transcendental meditation to The Movement Of Spiritual Awareness whose leader, John Rogers, helped compose one of the album's tracks. "The word 'light' refers to the awareness of the presence of God as an ongoing loving reality," Wilson says.

The person most responsible for producing the new album was not Brian Wilson, but Bruce Johnston, who both facially and vocally reminds one of the Kennedys. Johnston recalled how he originally became a Beach Boy. "Glen Campbell had already replaced Brian as a touring member of the band, but he had some solo work to do one weekend. Mike called me because he was aware that I knew a lot of musicians who would be anxious to play with the band that particular weekend.

"However, i couldn't find anyone. I even called our present bass player, Ed Carter, but he was going to graduate college in three months and was worried that he might join the band and not get his degree. So I just joined on a temporary basis, and it stretched out for seven more years."

AT the end of that time, mounting tensions within the group led to a unanimous vote that ousted Johnston from the Beach Boys. I asked Bruce if he still harbored any ambivalent feelings toward the group for his dismissal. "God, I really don't know," grimaced the lantern-jawed musician, trying to avoid answering the question in front of Carl. "See, I've made so much money and have done so many things since then (like working with Elton John and Art Garfunkel, and winning a 1977 Grammy

Dennis Wilson

14

Award for his composition *I Write The Songs*), that it doesn't bother me anymore. I figure that fate has a master plan for all of us. I had to get pulled out of the band to write some songs. I feel really positive about everything because I didn't realize how much I had learned, especially about vocal arranging, and when I was out on my own, I learned a lot about how the music business operates as well as some valuable production techinques. So it's enabled me to come back to the band a thousand times stronger."

As to his own contribution to the new album, Bruce tends to shy away from being called the producer. "We all really produced it," he explains. "I just feel like I organized everybody. At the beginning of the project the band was having some problem getting it off the ground, and they said, 'Wouldn't it be nice to get Bruce involved again.' The times have changed since the sixties, and perhaps Brian's productions are too short compared to what people are now accustomed to. But apart from that, Brian himself had called me and said, 'God, I've been smoking cigarettes, I can't sing high. Why don't you come down to Florida and just sing on the album.' It all sort of evolved from that."

Lead vocalist Mike Love, speaking several days later from his California-based production company, Lovesongs, was generous in his appraisal of Bruce's value to the band. "Bruce is so intimately knowlegeable about the group's strengths and weaknesses that he's been able to act as kind of an arranger and a funnel for all our different elements. That's why the album is a lot stronger than the last few, because we have someone who's outside, objective and very

Mike Love and Carl Wilson in concert after 18 years together.

Love: "Not everything should sound like Surfer Girl.*"*

skillful—and also aware of how the group works both harmonically as well as personality wise."

DESPITE the group's apparent satisfaction with Bruce's work, the obvious question is why he, and not Brian Wilson, produced the album. Love offers this explanation: "Brian's not really motivated anymore. It's a tremendous responsibility being responsible for all aspects of a recording project, although Brian is still involved musically to the point of writing and singing as well as arranging, but he doesn't have the follow-through of execution that he used to. When he cures himself of that, he should return to doing all the great things he's capable of. There's still no one better at structuring our harmonies or producing our records than Brian."

Despite Brian's well-publicized "comeback" of 1976, which has yet to live up to its expectations, the troubled musician's lack of involvement with the project was precipitated by the recent separation of his wife of 15 years. "In 1976, Brian was in a really healthy time, relatively speaking," relates Carl. "He's had a rough time recently, but is sort of on the upside of it once again."

Brian's only real contribution to the new album has been his singing on a few tracks. His song, *Good Timin'*, which was co-written by Carl, was actually composed four years ago, and the original track for *Shortnin' Bread*, was actually a leftover from the **15 Big Ones** of three years ago. Carl is more adamant than Mike at defending his older brother's lack of involvement. "Brian has a knack for getting a whole lot done in a relatively short time, so he doesn't have to hang around the studios during the

The backbeat of Disco has given the band a chance to stretch out.

GROOVES 79

15

recording of an album as much as Bruce and I do to get a lot of input into it. I really like the feeling of *Good Timin'*. It was a lot of fun mixing that track. We used a lot of echo on the voices and the track has a nice feeling to it. Mike's song *Sumahama* is really neat also. Bruce and I had a lot of fun doing the background parts in Japanese."

THE direct inspiration for the song was, in fact, Mike's lady, Sumako Kelley, who is of Oriental descent. "Sumako had told me this romantic story about her mother and father in Japan. I was driving home one evening from L.A. after seeing her, thinking about the story she had just told me, and "Suma" is this place known as a lovers' leap. Since the time I wrote the song, Sumako and I have gotten engaged and it looks like we'll be getting married in the Orient later this year."

The one cut on the album which has engendered the most controversy among Beach Boys cultists is the 11 minute disco remake of *Here Comes The Night*, which was originally done on the **Wild Honey** album 12 years ago. Were The Beach Boys influenced by the Bee Gees incredible resurgence of popularity in that format to go disco themselves? "It was just in the air for us to do that song in disco," says Carl, adding, "I just love the Bee Gees voices. Barry's voice just kills me."

Comments Bruce, "Using that format gave us an opportunity to expand our musical horizons. I don't think we're necessarily going to jump on the disco bandwagon, but it gives us a chance to stretch out."

"COME on Bruce; admit it. It's a showoff record, "quips Carl. Bruce quickly echos Carl's sentiments. "A lot of disco records are recorded and edited long. We cut ours long originally."

But didn't redoing an old song demonstrate a lack of inspiration within the group to come up with a totally new hit single? Bruce obviously didn't agree. "Good songs do not age," he steadfastly maintains. "Ya gotta remember, if something is good once, it'll always be good, regardless of it's age."

I remarked to Carl how at the previous evening's concert, when Mike had mentioned the word "disco" in the introduction of the song, most of the audience responded with a series of boos and catcalls. Did he feel this was the general consensus among Beach Boys fans? "I think those were pretty strong fans who booed. They probably have a certain feeling for a particular type of music that we're normally associated with, either the real arty stuff from the **Pet Sounds** era, or the lighter surfing things."

MIKE: "If some hard-core Beach Boys fans don't like or understand it because they think everything we do should sound like *Surfer Girl* or *Barbara Ann*, then there are different elements on the new album which should please them as much as *Here Comes The Night* pleases a disco audience. The fact that the song has created some controversy is good because it means that it didn't go unnoticed."

The album is also the group's first for James Guercio's Caribou label. Guercio, who is the manager and producer of Chicago, is also a longtime fan of the Beach Boys, with whom he has occasionally played bass. "For some time we'd wanted to be affiliated with CBS, which distributes Caribou," admits Carl. "So through Jim and our business people, we put the deal together."

Carl still faults their former record label (Warners) for their lack of commercial success in the '70s, which spawned only one hit single. "In 1970 we gave Warners an album called **Sunflower** which was a beautiful album and it was not promoted *at all*," says Carl. "Then we gave them some records, where perhaps the quality wasn't up to the standards people had come to expect from us, but they still should have sold a lot better than they did. **Surf's Up** was a really good album, and **Holland** had some nice moments on it as well."

EXPLAINS Carl of this period. "We were a lot weaker then. The general mood of the times was against us, and it was a real shaky time for us."

I inquired as to what was the lowest ebb of their stormy career. "Mitchell, South Dakota," announced Bruce proudly, while several other people in the room burst out laughing. "I gotta' tell you about this. We played a place there called The Corn Palace on Thanksgiving Day, 1969, and Mike was driving one of the station wagons at 100 miles an hour like a maniac trying to make the date on time, while I was eating turkey off the dashboard. When we finally got there, only about 50 people were in the audience. It was crazy."

Since that time, of course, the Beach Boys have re-established themselves as one of the world's biggest concert attractions. On record, the band may not be as strong as they were in their glory days, simply because the world they sang about no longer exists.

"It's possible that we could continue for another five years, although we probably can go on for as long as we want," Carl said. "As to how long that might be, I can't give you any set date."

What did he feel would ultimately break up the band? "If it stops working for us as individuals and I no longer get satisfaction from doing it, and being with the band is no longer important to my life, then I will do something else for a living." He paused to consider the gravity of his last statement while looking at the future with a furrowed brow and quickly decided, "However, I'd just like to add to what I just said that since I *love* what I'm doing so much, I'm gonna be hanging in there for awhile."

They may be grey, bearded and paunchy, but fans 20 years their junior are filling stadiums for the Beach Boys.

For the first time in years, the genius of The Beach Boys comes to Light.

The Beach Boys are five of the most talented musical minds of our time—all in one group.

And now here's the most solid evidence in years of their special brilliance.

"L.A. (Light Album)" includes Brian and Mike's "Here Comes the Night" in a tour-de-force version. It's got Brian and Carl's much written about (but never before released) "Good Timin'." Plus Al's "Lady Lynda." Mike's "Sumahama." Dennis' "Baby Blue" and "Love Surrounds Me." And some of Carl's absolutely best songs ever: "Full Sail," "Angel Come Home" (sung by Dennis) and "Goin' South."

All of it is co-produced by Grammy winner (and former Beach Boy) Bruce Johnston.*

This is The Beach Boys album everyone's been waiting for. You'll be turning people on to "L.A. (Light Album)" for months to come.

The Beach Boys "L.A. (Light Album)." On Caribou Records and Tapes.

* Produced by Bruce Johnston. The Beach Boys and James William Guercio, except "Here Comes the Night" produced by Bruce Johnston and Curt Becher. Distributed by CBS Records. © 1979 CBS Inc.

BEACH BOYS

WARNER/REPRISE

WORD ASSOCIATION TIME: I say "summer" and you say... right, "**The Beach Boys**." My fellow BB fans will be as pleased as I was to learn that

the golden Boys have been back in the studio, with **Brian Wilson** again assuming an avidly active role in writing, producing and performing. The result: a fat stack of new tracks, some of them rock oldies, some of them new originals. Brian and **Mike Love** dropped in the other day to play the home-office folks some samples of The Beach Boys' new Brother/Reprise album 15 *Big Ones* (there are 15 tunes), which is slated for late June, a release that will coincide nicely with the group's summer plans: an American tour running all of July as well as late August and early September (early August will find them in Europe) and a network TV special that will air on August 5.

The few minutes of music we heard were suggestive in style and spirit of The Beach Boys of *Pet Sounds* and *Sunflower* — in other words, wonderful. There were oldies ("Blueberry Hill" and "Rock and Roll Music" — the latter should be out as a single when you read this) and newies (no titles just yet). If there have been any doubts that this is a working, writing, living band — as well as a monumentally successful concert attraction — those doubts will be washed out with this summer's Beach Boys tide. "The beach," as **Timothy White** wrote in his recent Crawdaddy article on Brian & Co., "is back."

Hang 10 Again

The Beach Boys cut their first hit record the same year that most college freshmen were born. Eighteen years later, those good vibrations can still pack 'em in.

It's a warm spring evening on campus, and the air in the packed arena seems charged with electricity. Midterms are over, and the mood is that of a Friday-night party on a mammoth scale. Students dressed in everything from faded jeans to the latest disco synthetics fill the stands and crowd the arena floor. Pockets of teenagers also dot the audience, along with groups of older graduate students and professors. Everyone buzzes with anticipation.

Suddenly the lights go out and the crowd roars. Shadowy figures mount the stage, moving amid flashlight beams and the red lights of amps and electronic gear. Seconds tick by . . . or is it minutes? Time seems suspended as the cheering and applause reach fever pitch.

"LADIES AND GENTLEMEN," booms a voice over the microphone, "WOULD YOU PLEASE WELCOME . . . FROM HAWTHORNE, CALIFORNIA . . . THE BEACH BOYS!"

The stage explodes in bright, multicolored lights as the group churns into its opening number. Lead singer Mike Love, decked out in tight white slacks, a Hawaiian shirt, and a white cap, struts across the stage surveying the wild throng that's already clapping and pulsating to the beat. He grins, points out toward the crowd, and lets go:

"Well, East Coast girls are hip,

I really dig those styles they wear . . ."

Instant pandemonium reigns. The Beach Boys have come to town.

* * *

It was 1961 when the Beach Boys—Carl, Dennis, and Brian Wilson, their cousin Mike Love, and their neighbor Al Jardine had their first hit record. That was the year of John F. Kennedy's inauguration, the year when most of today's college freshmen were busy being born. By 1963, still a full year before anyone had heard of the Beatles, the Beach Boys were firmly entrenched on top of the national charts with a string of hit songs like "Surfin' U.S.A.," "Little Deuce Coupe," "Be True to Your School," and "Surfer Girl."

But the group didn't only sell records—it became a social force. The Beach Boys articulated the youthful appeal of the California mystique: a carefree, sunsplashed mosaic of sand, surf, fast cars, and endless summers. In the early '60s, Surf City became the cultural nucleus of American youth. *Everyone* wanted to be in California.

Today the Beach Boys stand alone as the great survivors, the only early-'60s rock band to reach the threshold of the '80s with its original lineup intact. It hasn't been easy. There have been a host of personal problems and intragroup battles over the years. Hardest of all to weather was the stormy cultural tumult of the late '60s, a period that saw the Beach Boys branded irrelevant and rejected by fans and fellow musicians alike. But they hung on, won back their old fans, and now boast a huge following that spans generations.

"The amazing thing about the Beach Boys," says Carl Wilson, "is that we're sort of caught in a time warp. Time and age are no longer reference points. We have our own energy stream, and our audience just plugs into it from wherever they happen to be."

At 32, Carl is the youngest Beach Boy. He's a quiet, soft-spoken fellow, and it's hard to believe that he's spent over half his life as a rock star. When it all started, he was only 14.

"I went back to Hawthorne a couple of years ago," he says, reminiscing as he stretches out in an overstuffed hotel lobby chair. "It was weird. Our house seemed real little. Somebody across the street was out front working on a car. When I was in high school a friend of mine who lived there used to do that. So I walked over—and it was the same guy! I realized then that I'd come quite a distance since high school. We all have. We were really just five dummies starting out, with no idea of what we were getting into. We just sang."

In fact, as the Wilson boys were growing up, the whole family sang. Their father Murray, a businessman, was a part-time songwriter, and their mother Audree liked to get everyone together for some vocalizing. It wasn't long before the teenage Wilson brothers progressed from these family sessions to Everly Brothers- and Four Freshmen-style harmonies. It was Brian, the oldest brother, who got the idea of grafting that vocal style to a Chuck Berry beat.

"It was a bizarre blend at the time, but it seemed to work," recalls Carl. In 1961, with encouragement from their parents, the boys formed a group with Al Jardine and Mike Love. Al, a good friend and football teammate of Brian's in high school, was due to start college that fall. He and Brian were both 18. Cousin Mike, 19, was working at a gas station. Dennis, 16, and Carl, 14, both attended Hawthorne High. The group practiced in the Wilson basement, with Brian on bass, Dennis on drums, and Carl and Al on guitars.

One day Dennis, who was an avid surfer, suggested to Brian that the group do a song with a surfing theme. Though he'd never hung 10 himself, Brian wrote "Surfin'" with some help from Mike. Brian's father took a tape of the song around to various music publishers he knew, finally getting a bite from Candix, a now-defunct Los Angeles record company.

The group recorded the song in 10 minutes, with Brian beating on a plastic trash can to accompany the boys' harmonies. "Surfin'" became an instant local hit and dented the national charts enough to get the group signed by Capitol Records that fall. "Surfin' Safari," their first song for Capitol, struck national gold, and the Beach Boys were on their way.

Surfing struck America like a tsunami. The beach became the collective teenage venue, and the Beach Boys were suddenly the pied pipers of a generation.

"I think people's imaginations had as much to do with it as we did," says Al. "Especially if you're landlocked, the beach is something you can dream about."

Carl Wilson is equally modest about the group's early success. "The times were just right for us, I guess," he says. "Our songs just reflected what it was like to live in California at that time."

Many of those reflections were things that *all* teenagers, landlocked or not, could directly relate to—from cruising the hamburger stand to summer romance and the Friday-night football game. Hit followed hit, and songs like "Shut Down," "409," "Barbara Ann," and "Fun, Fun, Fun" flooded the airwaves.

"Suburban teenage folk songs," Mike Love has called them, "inseparable from the white middle-class karma." Almost all of them were written by Brian, who managed to get the group complete artistic control in the studio. This was no small feat in the early '60s, especially for such young musicians.

Brian set a precedent by taking the act away from Capitol to different studios," explains Al. "He just couldn't work with their producers, he wanted to do it himself. It was great for us, and really was the luckiest thing that ever happened to Capitol. We would walk in with finished masters. We were handing them gold on a platter."

With each succeeding album (there were seven by 1964, when Brian was still only 21), the arrangements took on new richness, complexity, and innovation. Brian was heavily influenced by the production concept of Phil Spector, whose records with the Ronettes and the Crystals made use of layers of instrumentation combined for a wall-of-sound effect. Brian melded the Beach Boys' polished harmonies to these production techniques, creating pop masterpieces like "Help Me Rhonda," "California Girls," and "I Get Around."

In early 1964, however, a new force swept onto the music scene. The Beatles turbocharged the nation's teenagers in a way that made even the Beach Boys gape.

"We were on tour in Australia at the time," recalls Carl, "and I remember getting back and hearing 'I Wanna Hold Your Hand' every 15 minutes on the radio. I was blown away."

So were the record companies, especially Capitol, which had managed to bag the

Beatles. Although the Beach Boys kept producing hits as well, there was suddenly great pressure on the group to churn out singles and keep pace with the Lads from Liverpool.

In addition to doing almost all of the writing and producing for the Beach Boys, Brian Wilson had to cope with a demanding tour schedule and increasing deafness in his right ear. He was innately quiet and shy, and in late 1964 he finally buckled under the combined pressures weighing on him. Brian quit touring with the group and

On campus, vintage Beach Boys' music pours from student centers, Greek houses and dormitory halls.

went home to cool out and concentrate on writing. He was replaced on the road by a succession of musicians that included Glen Campbell, Daryl Dragon (the Captain of Captain and Tenille), and Bruce Johnston.

Although "retired" as a performer, Brian kept on writing hits and producing, sometimes arranging and recording entire instrumental tracks of albums for the group while they were on tour. When they returned they would have to learn the new songs in the studio so that they could fill in the vocals.

"It got hard to adjust to that, because Brian's new music began getting really personal and far out. It took a good deal of adapting," explains Al.

Brian's new music began in earnest in late 1965 with the *Pet Sounds* album, which many considered the first concept album to be musically thematic. On cuts like "God Only Knows," "Sloop John B," and "Wouldn't It Be Nice," the harmonies and wall-of-sound orchestrations were more elaborate than ever.

This album was followed by the monumental single "Good Vibrations," which took six months of work in five studios to

complete. Released in the fall of 1966, the song, which Brian Wilson called his "pocket symphony," wove a myriad of unlikely instruments (cello, theremin, and harpsichord, for instance) together with intricate vocal harmonies and mood changes. Although *Pet Sounds* had sold sluggishly (it was the first Beach Boys album that had no surfing or car songs), "Good Vibrations" topped the charts for weeks. The Beach Boys' star seemed still on the rise and brighter than ever. But things were about to change drastically.

By the next year, 1967, a cultural revolution was shifting the concerns of youth in America. Gone were the sunkissed, halcyon days of endless summer.

"Now we'll never have to listen to surf music again," said Jimi Hendrix when he burst onto the scene at the '67 Monterey Pop Festival. Music had become an important expression of social change—and suddenly the Beach Boys seemed very adolescent and irrelevant.

It wasn't as if the group remained stagnant or oblivious to what was happening. They grew beards and long hair, dabbled in drugs and Transcendental Meditation, played at antiwar benefits. And their music continued to evolve and to express themes that were more topical, even mystical. But while other fans, such as those of the Beatles, followed their groups through such changes, the Beach Boys found themselves swiftly deserted.

"It was really a strange time," reflects Carl Wilson. "Here we were, growing and changing along with everyone else, but the group just wasn't accepted. We were locked into the surfing thing."

"A lot of the problem was how we were packaged," says Al Jardine. "The record companies refused to promote our new stuff, so it never came across. And since we were basically a vocal group, we didn't have the latitude to get into, say, acid rock or heavy instrumental stuff."

As the '60s moved into the '70s, the Beach Boys continued to tour (sans Brian), much of the time overseas where they were better received. But they were beset by numerous personal problems and group conflicts. Various marriages and divorces took place. Dennis became involved with the Manson clan for a time, and Carl, busted by the FBI for draft dodging, struggled through a six-year court battle to win conscientious-objector status.

Though they kept producing albums during these years (among them *Wild Honey, Smiley Smile, Holland,* and *Sunflower*), most sold poorly. The group went through four record companies. Brian still wrote most of the music, but he rarely strayed from his house in West Los Angeles, content to sleep and spend short hours composing music on a piano that sat in a huge sandbox in the middle of his living room. Heavily into drugs and hamburgers, Brian ballooned to a weight of 250 pounds. By the end of 1972 he had retreated to his
continued on page 102

Tim, you've got carte blanche with the Beach Boys," said the publicist over the phone. "Pictures, interviews, whatever you want. It's all set."

I was skeptical. Six months earlier, the same publicist had set up an interview for me with Aerosmith in New York. I had flown up there expecting a leisurely afternoon session in their hotel. Instead I got 10 minutes in a crowded Madison Square Garden equipment room, with only one band member. At midnight. And for that I'd had to struggle through three days of hassles and runarounds from the group's Palace Guard, an abrasive coterie of promoters, managers and other Aerosmith functionaries. Every big band has its own set of PG's, whose function is to coordinate tours and insulate its group from the outside world. I wasn't psyched for another siege.

"Won't happen again, Tim," the publicist assured me. "That was a bad mix-up on my part. This time will be smooth."

Friday, a month later: Our photographer, Charlie, was signed up to accompany me to the interview and the evening's concert. When I called early in the day, the Beach Boys' road manager (whom I'll call Abraham) sounded open and friendly. Yes, he had spoken to the publicist in New York. "Listen, Carl's got to do some radio interviews. You want to come along?"

That sounded appealing. Interviews often flow better if you have a chance to just shoot the breeze first. Besides, I'd grown up in Los Angeles, and the Beach Boys had been a major force in my early life. I had even shed blood for them in a fifth-grade fight against Beatle fans in 1964, and I was hoping for a chance to converse informally with at least one of them. "What time can we have a group interview?" I asked.

There was a pause. "Well, I'll have to work that out. Later on in the day."

I felt a creeping sense of dread.

A couple of hours later, Charlie and I piled into a limousine along with Carl Wilson, Abraham, and two record-company promo people.

"Do you do this a lot?" I asked Carl.

"Yeah. I like radio stations," he said. "All those control rooms and dials. It's fun." Suddenly Abraham broke in.

"Why don't you do some of your questions now? Get in some extra time?"

So much for informal conversation. Suddenly I was beginning an interview while packed into the back of a limo with five people. So much for shooting the breeze.

Back at the hotel Carl and I continued the interview for a while. But Al and Mike weren't there. "They must be at the health club or something," Abraham said. "You can get them before the show tonight. Plenty of time. Be there at eight, you'll have press passes at the gate."

He whisked Carl off, leaving Charlie and me sitting there in the hotel lobby. Acute anxiety struck. I'd been through this scene before—getting the shaft, in installments.

Friday, 7:30 p.m.: Charlie and I stood at the press gate of Stokely Athletic Center on the University of Tennessee campus.

"Sorry. Your names aren't on the list," said a PG who stood there holding a clipboard.

BACKSTAGE WITH THE PALACE GUARD:

"You'll have press passes at the gate," said the Beach Boys' road manager—then he was gone. Acute anxiety struck me. I'd been through this scene before— getting the shaft, in installments.

"This can't be happening," Charlie said. "I saw this on *Saturday Night Live.*"

After 15 minutes of haggling and phone calls, we had the press passes. But after making our way through the bowels of the arena to the Beach Boys' dressing room, we were accosted by a small, mousy PG (probably an apprentice).

"Where did you get those?" he demanded pointing, to our stage passes. From Abraham, we told him. "Abraham gave you those? You're not supposed to have those!" he exclaimed incredulously. He stormed off, quickly returning with another, larger PG.

"We've got a special press room upstairs," the PGs told us. "You have to go up there. And we're going to take those passes away and give you these instead." The PGs assured us that we could get on stage for photos with the replacement passes. We made the exchange, resolving to blast our way to the stage if necessary.

The special press room was a musty classroom off one of the hallways upstairs. Empty beer bottles and milk cartons were scattered about. Large puddles covered the floor. "I had an ROTC class in here once," Charlie said.

By 8:30, no one had arrived. We decided to wander around backstage for a while, and soon noticed several *really* large PGs—bouncers, who were probably former Dallas Cowboys. They eyed

us suspiciously, champing at the bit of restraint. So much for storming the stage.

"I feel like an intruder," I said.

"Worse," said Charlie. "I feel like a groupie."

The arena had been filled since eight o'clock, and the opening act (Ian Matthews) was playing. As it began to get close to nine, I cornered the mousy PG, who claimed he knew nothing about our scheduled interview.

"Talk to Abraham," he said.

"Where is he?"

"Abraham will come to you," he replied. It sounded like a Biblical prophecy. Charlie inquired about getting the band together in the press room for some group pictures when they arrived.

"Get the whole band together? No way! Such things never happen," said the mouse, striding off.

It was 9:30 when Abraham arrived with the Beach Boys in tow. They immediately headed for the dressing room downstairs. We tried to follow, but our new passes wouldn't get us past the six club-and-gun-laden policemen blocking the stairs. Fifteen minutes later, Abraham returned with Mike Love. Accompanied by a TV crew, they zoomed past us and into the special press room, slamming the door behind them. I pounded on the door. Abraham opened it enough to stick his head out; icy hostility was in his eyes.

"Off limits, man," he growled.

"Wait a minute. What happened to our eight o'clock interview?" I demanded.

"We couldn't make it. C'mon, get out of here. You can talk to Love for a couple minutes when the TV is through." He slammed the door. I was seething now. When he emerged, Charlie and I cornered him. Philosophies on press relations were exchanged in heated tones.

"You're pushing me, man, and I don't need it," Abraham snapped. "You can talk to Al or Mike tomorrow morning, and that's it."

Charlie inquired about getting some pictures on stage. "No cameras on stage, ever," Abraham declared. "It freaks out the band. You can take pictures near the stage, for the first two songs. *And don't make me come out after you.*"

He reentered the press room, and a moment later escorted the television crew— and their rather large camera—onto the stage. Then the house lights went out and the Beach Boys filed by.

Postscript: The next morning I was able to talk to Al Jardine. He couldn't have been nicer. Halfway through our session, Dennis and Brian Wilson (the two Beach Boys who *never* give interviews) wandered by and stopped to say hello.

"Want to interview?" Al asked. Well, they were on their way out, Brian explained.

"You shoulda come by earlier," he said. ∎

continued from page 100 bedroom, the Howard Hughes of rock 'n' roll. He stayed there for most of the next three years, and the Beach Boys made no new albums.

During that period, however, a strange thing began to happen. Perhaps because they were bored, perhaps because they were disillusioned with the rigors of the protest era, people who had once rejected the Beach Boys longed to feel carefree again. Although they were now in college—even, by the early '70s, through college—they started listening to the old songs once again. And their younger brothers and sisters (and children), often hearing the music for the first time, were exposed to an age of innocence that, growing up in the shadow of Vietnam and Watergate, they had never known.

Sensing a gold mine out there, Capitol Records released a two-record set of vintage, pre-1965 Beach Boys songs in 1974. The album, *Endless Summer*, didn't merely sell well—it went through the roof, zooming to Number One position in a matter of weeks. The group was in demand as never before, especially on college campuses where the 10-year-old songs were permeating dorm halls and fraternity and sorority quads. Somewhat astonished, the Beach Boys played to packed houses across the country and set several single-concert

attendance records.

"At first it was really a battle," recalls Carl. "We wanted to play our newer stuff and they didn't want to hear it. But finally we just accepted that people like a lot of the things we did. We don't want to invalidate any of it. When you see what those old songs can do to an audience . . . it's just pure energy. It's great."

"The old songs just have a special exuberance," says Al. "I think they're national treasures. And now that we're back in the studio regularly, people are picking up on our new stuff, too."

The *new* new stuff. Since 1976 the Beach Boys have turned out no fewer than four new albums. Once again, the driving force has been Brian Wilson. In 1976 he finally decided to get his act together. With the help of a psychiatrist and an athletic trainer, Brian emerged from his bedroom, swore off drugs, and sweated off pounds. He also took the Beach Boys back into the studio for the first time in three years. The resulting album, *15 Big Ones*, sold well, and the group went on to do a television special that summer with *Saturday Night Live*'s Dan Aykroyd and John Belushi. (The highlight was a skit in which Brian was arrested for "failure to surf.")

Since 1976, it's all been upward for the group—and there's no end in sight. The latest LP, *The Light Album*, is heading for gold, and another album is due out in the fall. Four of the Beach Boys are planning

solo albums, a film on the group is in production, and they continue to tour—with Brian now—for two to three months each year. Concert audiences are responding to the newer songs enthusiastically, for a change—even to a (heaven forbid) *disco* tune the group recorded on *The Light Album*.

"The disco song was an experiment that we had a lot of fun with," says Al. "It's not going to be a pattern, though. What you're seeing with disco is the pendulum swinging back from the counterculture, where it wasn't cool to value possessions or appearance. It'll swing back again, and the Beach Boys will hopefully stay in the middle somewhere. We plan to be around for a long time yet."

*   *   *

The concert's over now, and as the students file out, the air still rings with the last strains of the rollicking encore. Near the stage stand several sorority girls who don't want to leave yet. They're dressed in striped surfer shirts, and they're singing:

"We'll all be gone for the summer,
We're on safari to stay.
Tell the teacher we're surfin',
Surfin' U.S.Aaaaaaaaaaay . . ." ∎

Staff writer Tim Smight, a Los Angeles native, spent his formative years memorizing the lyrics to Beach Boys albums.

Classics of the Sixties: Nothing Beats the Real Thing

In these times of inflated record prices, old cutouts of '60s albums are often the best buys that a record store has to offer. Some classic albums sell for as little as $1.98, unopened. Many others can be purchased at garage sales and at used-record stores for even less than that.

Bargain hunting for '60s records can be aesthetically pleasing, too. Rarely does a new version of a song do justice to the original. Imitation may be the sincerest form of flattery, but nothing beats the real thing. Here are some of the classics:

The Beatles. Lots of people will argue with me, but for my money, the best Beatles records are their old ones. Their sound on those old LPs is bursting with exuberance and passion. John Lennon's vocals are the driving point that the rest of the band hammers home. It's still possible to find their first American album, *Meet the Beatles* on the Capitol label. It's a steal if you can get it, featuring several old rhythm and blues standards that the Beatles were weaned on before they made it big. Two of their greatest-hits collections are also relatively easy to find: *The Beatles: 1962-1966* (Apple) and *Rock 'n' Roll Music* (Capitol).

The Rolling Stones. *Some Girls* (London), issued in 1978, showed the Stones in fine form after several disappointing

albums this decade. But fans who picked up their earlier records will be pleasantly surprised. In the 1970s, Mick Jagger's nastiness was something of an enigma. Why would someone so rich complain so much? But on his earlier albums, his nihilistic stance seems less of a pose. Any of the Stones' three earliest greatest-hits collections is well worth owning: *Big Hits (High Tide and Green Grass)*, *Through the Past Darkly*, and *Hot Rocks* (London).

The Animals. Eric Burdon, their lead singer was the Johnny Rotten of the '60s. Burdon was a grungy, rat-faced little jerk who seemed destined to be a grease monkey except for the fact that he could

sing a rhythm and blues song better than anyone else around. The band's playing was as street-tough as his vocal style. Their records are increasingly hard to find, but eminently worth the effort of looking for them—especially *Animalization* (Columbia) and *Best of the Animals* (MGM).

The Yardbirds. A seminal blues band that spawned guitar greats Jimmy Page, Eric Clapton, and Jeff Beck, the Yardbirds were the most underrated band of the '60s. They produced only two American hits, "Heart Full of Soul" and "For Your Love," but their early albums are chock-full of great rhythm and blues classics. Albums to look for are *Having a Rave Up With the Yardbirds* and *Greatest Hits*. (Epic).

Motown. Almost any of the greatest-hits packages on Motown and its subsidiary labels (Tamla, Gordy, Soul) are fantastic records. But any other old Motown records may be a disappointment. In the '60s Motown was preoccupied with selling singles, not LPs. So they usually just wrapped hit singles around a lot of filler and sold them as albums. Their greatest-hits records, however, are certifiably wonderful. The best of the lot are *The Four Tops Greatest Hits* and *Diana Ross and the Supremes' Greatest Hits*. ∎

PERFORMANCE

The International Touring Talent Weekly Newspaper.

Volume 15, No. 49   April 25, 1986 $3.50

The Beach Boys Surf Into Their 25th Year

Special Pullout Supplement: 1986 Promoter/Club Directory

TOPS in PERFORMANCE: ZZ Top   *Gross of the Week: Grateful Dead*

Sunkist® is proud to celebrate 25 years of Good Vibrations.

Halfway between Heaven and California sits a world...made of the spirit, the images and sweet, rich harmonies unique to America's Band—The Beach Boys. In this world, the anthem is Good Vibrations and Sunkist is proud to be among the voices who sing it. We are prouder still that The Beach Boys have made Sunkist® the Official Sponsor of this spectacular 25th Anniversary Tour. We invite you to have Fun, Fun, Fun as The Beach Boys take you on a tour of their special world. Wouldn't it be nice if it lasted forever...

A Sunkist Celebration.

© 1986 Sunkist Growers, Inc.
Sunkist is a registered trademark of Sunkist Growers, Inc.

The Bruce Johnston Interview:
"We're Basically The Boys Of Summer"

by Bob Grossweiner

PACIFIC PALISADES, Calif.: In addition to being keyboardist/singer with the Beach Boys, Bruce Johnston is best known as the writer of the song "I Write The Songs," which Barry Manilow had a number one pop hit with in 1976. Johnston was able to do a solo album because of the song, and with the $100,000 advance, he was able to furnish his home.

"I'm a fan of songwriting," says the 41-year-old native of Chicago, who joined the Beach Boys in 1965. "Nothing matters until the song is written, neither the studio technology nor the ability of the artist to deliver. You can't deliver until the song is written."

One of Johnston's biggest disappointments in music was the breakup of the Eagles, whom he considered "The Beach Boys, Part II" because of their songwriting and singing ability. And perhaps that has a lot to say about the Beach Boys because not only is their music fun, but the Beach Boys were one of the first rock groups to concentrate on harmonies.

The Beach Boys are a tightly knit band. It was tragic that Dennis Wilson drowned a few years ago, but the Beach Boys never considered quitting because of the death. On the afternoon of the press conference when the Beach Boys said they would halt touring for a few months, they went into the studio to record new material.

The Beach Boys were recently inducted into the *PERFORMANCE* Touring Hall of Fame by the 1985 PERFORMANCE Awards. Johnston was honored that the group won. "Our operation is not sleazy at all," he reflects upon the group's professional reputation. "Our vendors do not get stiffed. Our bills get paid."

PERFORMANCE: Have the individual members of the Beach Boys developed areas of specialization when it comes to touring and recording?

BRUCE JOHNSTON: Over the years, everybody has developed a special strength. On the basic touring level, Mike (Love) has always been interested in the routing of a tour. Al (Jardine) has always been interested in the overall costs of a tour so that the nets could be acceptable. Carl (Wilson) has been instrumental in the quality of the sound systems, the acoustics of the hall, and the musicians who accompany us. Carl also thinks about recording the most. Brian (Wilson) specializes in writing songs, and creating arrangements to songs we sing that we don't write. He doesn't think about the road. He has an unusual rule about the road: He can go out or stay home. It's his choice. He designed himself out of the band as early as 1963. That's how I wound

25 Years of Fun, Fun, Fun

SOUTHERN CALIFORNIA: The Beach Boys epitomize the beach, surfin', cars and girls in songdom. But it is surprising to note that only Dennis Wilson was a surfer.

The Beach Boys started primarily as a family group with Brian, Carl, and Dennis Wilson, their cousin Mike Love and their friend Al Jardine in 1961. In fact, Dennis was not part of his brothers' original group plans until his mother insisted that his brothers let him join. In 1965, Bruce Johnston joined the group as a touring replacement for Brian, who wrote himself out of the road group but could also get on stage any time he wished. Johnston left in 1972 and came back six years later. Thus the Beach Boys have had practically the original personnel throughout most of their career until Dennis' untimely drowning a few winters ago. The Beach Boys no longer all live in Southern California. Vocalist/guitarist Al Jardine resides in Arizona and Big Sur; vocalist/keyboardist Bruce Johnston lives in Pacific Palisades and is moving to Santa Barbara; vocalist Mike Love has houses in Santa Barbara and Los Angeles; vocalist/keyboardist/bassist Brian Wilson lives in Southern California; and vocalist/guitarist Carl Wilson resides in Colorado.

Surprisingly, the Beach Boys only have two gold singles, 1966's "Good Vibrations" and 1964's "I Get Around," which was certified 18 years later in 1982. One would have thought that the Beach Boys had many more million sellers, but most of their songs are golden nonetheless.

The Beach Boys, along with Bruce Springsteen, were the initial inductees into the PERFORMANCE Touring Hall of Fame as voted by the 1985 reader's poll. The Beach Boys are the granddaddy of American rock and roll groups with a clean cut image and familiar songs.

PERFORMANCE interviewed both Bruce Johnston and Mike Love among the group members — Brian, unfortunately, does not do interviews. ●

A look back at the early years

up in the Beach Boys in 1965 filling in for Brian. He did something pretty smart by incorporating me immediately into the recording process. Instead of me recreating his sound as my role in the band, I sang on "California Girls" in the studio and created my own identity.

PERFORMANCE: You left out your specialized role.

JOHNSTON: It's hard for me to say what my function is for the road.

PERFORMANCE: Then let's assume that I ask another band member the same question. What do you think he would say is your role?

JOHNSTON: Probably some creative mediator... What I like is that the guys in our band are singing the songs in the same keys when we recorded the songs origi-

cont'd on next page

cont'd from page 5

nally. The band has been around so long — other singers have been around as long and moved their keys down a key or two. If you don't have to do that, it's better to keep it as original as you can. We just did a "Good Vibrations" spot for Sunkist (the 1986 Silver Anniversary tour sponsor). We hadn't recorded the song since 1966, and we have the same voices. It sounds great. I can't go out into the audience and hear ourselves during a concert so I don't know what the audiences hear. But when you hear this spot on the radio, it's going to sound like us. We used our road band as well to make us sound like we do today.

Unless otherwise noted, all candid photographs of the Beach Boys are by Gilbert Head and Margaret Dowdle Head. PERFORMANCE extends its appreciation to the Heads for providing these photographs.

PERFORMANCE: What is the Beach Boys' current recording status?

JOHNSTON: We are out of our CBS (Caribou) deal. A major label is already negotiating with us. We got out of the deal so recently that we haven't had a meeting yet to discuss what we wanted to do when this call came in from a major, aggressive major, label with a very young president. We were very surprised and flattered. (Johnston emphatically claims that it is not Geffen Records.)

PERFORMANCE: How important is it for the group's longevity to have a current recording contract?

JOHNSTON: There's nothing better than to have a fabulous album and a single that are doing well. No matter how many hits we have had or how healthy the road is — and ours is a lot healthier than bands who have had multi-platinum albums — it's absolutely essential.

PERFORMANCE: How do you account for the Beach Boys' longevity considering that you have not had many hits over the past few years? And you probably have been more successful on the road in the past few years than ever before.

JOHNSTON: The songs that we sing which Brian wrote or arranged, like "Sloop John B," have an appeal and an uniqueness that holds up over the years. It also addresses an in-school demographic. No matter which way the music business has turned, people still go to school. No matter how cool they think they become, they still have to deal with a car to get to school, deal with getting to the beach, and deal with girls — all the basic things. No one else sings about it as straight forward as we do.

PERFORMANCE: So your concerts attract new fans as well as the old ones?

JOHNSTON: We may retain our old fans, but they don't necessarily come to the shows because we have about 80 percent of our audience under 25 years old. We're singing about their lives plus there's a continuing uniqueness to the records we sing. If the Beatles were still around and touring, their music would still have a similar appeal, but they might not have such a wide demographic.

PERFORMANCE: Was the incident in Washington, D.C., in 1983 when the then Interior Secretary James Watt cancelled your Independence Day concert by saying the Beach Boys attracted "undesirable elements," a blessing in disguise?

JOHNSTON: It was a booster shot. It reminded people who graduated from the Beach Boys into the world of having a career, a family and mortgages, who didn't attend concerts as regularly as when they were in school. It reminded them that some of their heroes were still around. We got a nice vote of support from them with their reaction.

PERFORMANCE: How often do the Beach Boys tour a year?

JOHNSTON: About a hundred dates a year. It has turned into a seasonal thing, a bit like baseball but a shorter season. We're basically the boys of summer. It seems to work really well with our music. We will go abroad once in a while. We will go to Australia for their summer, our winter. We play one club a year for three days at Harrah's in Lake Tahoe, which allows everybody to go skiing for three or four days. It's the best nightclub in the United States. It was

Bruce Johnston

built around artists; Bill Harrah was an artist oriented man.

PERFORMANCE: How popular are you around the world?

JOHNSTON: I think you have to be American to really understand the Beach Boys. It's like when Elton John and Rod Stewart tried to promote soccer matches in America. Americans still love their football. We sold out concerts in Europe where the people remained silent other than applauding at the end of the songs.

PERFORMANCE: What about Japan?

JOHNSTON: The last time we played Japan, it was with Heart and a few other bands outdoors. They had watched Woodstock and other concerts that took place outdoors, and they behaved looser than the first time we played there when it was like they elected who would applaud. It was funny.

The United States and Canada are best for us. We would sellout in England, but people there tend to think of us as an oldies group, like the Americans perceive the Four Seasons today, and with the audiences up a couple of waist sizes.

PERFORMANCE: You also play a lot of free outdoor festivals. Which do you prefer?

JOHNSTON: I would rather play in front of 4,000 people and do two shows on a good wood floor, but that's pretty rare since we have far bigger crowds than that. It's pretty heady and wonderful to play in front of really large crowds but it's not something I would like to do too much. Mike loves to be on the stage 24 hours a day singing, either in a club or on the Fourth of July in Washington, D.C.

cont'd on next page

San Diego Padres and The Beach Boys
1985 Sports/Concert Event - 58,000 *SELLOUT*

Alan Jardine

Mike Love

Carl Wilson

cont'd from page 7

27 Songs In A Set

PERFORMANCE: What are your most requested songs in concert?

JOHNSTON: We do 27 songs every night. We have "A," "B," and "C" sets so that we don't get bored. We have 350 songs in the library. We always do "Good Vibrations," "Surfin' U.S.A.," "Barbara Ann," and "Fun, Fun, Fun." A lot of songs go in and out. We could probably do three-to-four hour sets, but we do an hour-and-a-half set, which to me, is not long enough. We sing songs that are only about two-and-a-half minutes long.

I would rather do a two hour show with an intermission and without an opening act, but that isn't practical.

PERFORMANCE: Why?

JOHNSTON: My biggest complaint on the road is when the promoter takes a local act and uses them to open for us, which totally wipes out the ears of the audience. They get them for about $300, and the acts look like they're in mid-beginnings. A compatible newcomer is OK. Sometimes the agents are probably using up favors.

Corporate Sponsorships

PERFORMANCE: In 1985, the Beach Boys undertook their first corporate sponsorship for a tour with AMC's jeep division. . .

JOHNSTON: . . .it was really fun. . .

PERFORMANCE: . . .why is the group doing such sponsorships?

JOHNSTON: You mean why are corporations coming to us. It's because the linkage is really good. We appeal to people who like their products. It certainly aids in the tour promotion with the extra dollars tagged into ads giving us more exposure to when the event will be. Last year, it was exciting to give a jeep away every night and watch the people's reaction. They buy a $15 ticket to a show and someone walks out with a $10,000 jeep. It was a pretty good bargain.

PERFORMANCE: Why did you go with Sunkist this year?

JOHNSTON: They have been playing our music for the last seven years. They built a whole company around oranges and carbonation and our music. It seems appropriate in our 25 years to marry the two. Every can has had the words "good vibrations" on it for the past seven years.

PERFORMANCE: What are some of the touring plans for the group in the future?

JOHNSTON: In the future, we will work with Michel Colombier. We put together a Father's Day event with the Denver Symphony and the Beach Boys at Mile High Stadium. The night before, they sold out a show with the symphony for 3,500 people. We played the next afternoon, a Sunday, in front of 45,000 people. The Symphony played some of their lighter songs, like "Star Wars." Then we played for an hour, and then with the Symphony for a half-hour to test the waters. Then the Symphony did

cont'd on page 12

Johnston in concert

cont'd from page 10
another 20 minutes while fireworks were set off. It was a great event.

The Beach Boys will probably play with more symphonies in the future. That was our prototype. It was a half hour of music to see how it sounded, and it sounded great. We had 100 people in the symphony playing "Fun, Fun, Fun." A week before, we hired the Chicago Symphony Orchestra to rehearse the parts out in a studio.

I would like to do 10-15 dates a year like this, maybe some for charities. I would even like the Beach Boys to be a symphony's guest in the winter and drastically reduce our fee to cover just our expenses. I would love to do some of our more serious music, like "Heroes and Villians," and "Caroline No." We know it can work.

Charter Planes

PERFORMANCE: Do the Beach Boys prefer to bus or fly on tour?

JOHNSTON: Fly! I've never ever in my life been on a bus! The group bussed in 1963 and that was it. Flying is more efficient. We have a charter plane so it doesn't make sense to take a bus. So we base somewhere which gives the band a lot more rest. We charter a BAC 111 or a Vicount, a four-engine Turbo jet. It allows time during the day to get a nap, to work out of the hotel, to do business calls, and to be able to be reached by our families most of the time except for six or so hours a day

Beach Boys Set 100-Date Tour

NEW YORK: The Beach Boys' Silver Anniversary 100-date summer tour begins in Jacksonville, Fla., on May 31 and winds down on Labor Day Weekend, Sept. 2. Then the group will do spot dates in the Northwest in September and October with possible Australian and Eurpoean tours being considered.

According to Dennis Arfa, the group's responsible agent at William Morris, the Beach Boys will play approximately 75 percent of their shows outdoors, ideal party atmosphere for the group that promotes the beach, sun and surfing. A few outdoor festivals with crowds between 100,000-250,000 people are also expected with one already lined up for Charleston, W. Va. The Love Foundation, which promoted the Beach Boys' all-star extravaganzas in Philadelphia and Washington, D.C., in the past might be involved in some of these big festivals.

"The Beach Boys' music is timeless," says Arfa, who has booked the California group since 1980 when they were signed to his Home Run Agency. "Look at all the people who have recorded their music, like David Lee Roth ("California Girls") and Joan Jett (a forthcoming "Fun, Fun, Fun"). The Beach Boys are one of the few musical institutions of a sound that is still together. They're alive and well."

"The Beach Boys are California's child," adds Arfa. "They're America's child; they're America's band. They stand for beaches, surfing, partying. They're a fun band!" — **Bob Grossweiner**

Beach Boys Itinerary
BA: William Morris Agency

NS Halifax, Metro Centre	May 3
NB Moncton, Moncton Coliseum	May 4
NB Fredericton, Aitken Center	May 5
NF St. Johns, Memorial Stadium	May 7
CA San Diego, Jack Murphy Stadium	May 18
FL Jacksonville, Metropolitan Park	May 31

MS Biloxi, Gulf Coast Coliseum	June 1
TN Nashville, Herschell Greer Stadium	June 2
TN Memphis, Mud Island	June 4-5
AL Huntsville, Joe W. Davis Stadium	June 6
MO St. Louis, Muni	June 7
TX Dallas, Texas Stadium	June 8
OK Oklahoma City, All Sports Stadium	June 9
MI Marquette, Lakeview Arena	June 11
IL Rockford, Metro Center	June 12
OH Cincinnati, Kings Island	June 13
IN Indianapolis, Sports Music Center	June 14
OH Cleveland, Blossom Music Festival	June 15
NY Binghamton, Broome Co. Arena	June 18
MI Detroit, Pine Knob	June 19-20
PA York, Fairgrounds	June 21
NY Syracuse, State Fairgrounds	June 22
NY Saratoga Springs, PAC	June 23
NH Manchester, Arms Park	June 25
PQ Montreal, Man & His World/La Ronde	June 26
MA Boston, Great Woods Amphitheatre	June 27
NY Buffalo, War Memorial Stadium	June 28
MI Muskeegon, Lumbertown Music Festival (afternoon)	June 29
MI Charlevoix, Castle Farms (evening)	June 29
IA Sioux City, Roberts Stadium	July 1
MO Kansas City, Sandstone	July 2
NE Omaha, Rosenblatt Stadium	July 3
TBA	July 4
CA Costa Mesa, Pacific Amphitheatre	July 16
CA San Francisco, Shoreline Amphitheatre	July 17
CA Sacramento, TBA	July 18
CA Chico, Silver Dollar Fairgrounds (afternoon)	July 19
UT Salt Lake City, TBA (evening)	July 19
CO Denver, Red Rocks	July 20
ND Minot, Fair	July 21
WI Milwaukee, Alpine Valley	July 24
TX Houston, Astrodome	July 25
AR Ft. Smith, Harper Stadium	July 26
KS Wichita, Lawrence-Dumont Stadium	July 27
MO Lampe, Swiss Villa	July 28
IN Evansville, Mesker Theatre	July 30
ON Toronto, TBA	Aug. 1
PA Clearfield, Fair	Aug. 2
PA Pittsburgh, Civic Arena	Aug. 3
OH Columbus, State Fair	Aug. 4
TBA	Aug. 5-10
NJ Holmdel, GSAC	Aug. 11-12
NY Jones Beach, Marine Theatre	Aug. 14-15
CT Bridgeport, JFK Stadium	Aug. 16
MD Columbia, Merriweather Post Pavilion	Aug. 17
NY Jones Beach, (rain date)	Aug. 18
PA Erie, TBA	Aug. 19
PA Philadelphia, Mann Music Center	Aug. 20
KY Louisville, State Fair	Aug. 22
IA Des Moines, State Fair	Aug. 24
MN Minneapolis, State Fair	Aug. 25
SD Huron, State Fair	Aug. 26
IL Chicago, Poplar Creek	Aug. 27
GA Atlanta, Chastain Park	Aug. 29
WV Charleston, Riverfront Stage	Aug. 30
PA Allentown, Fair	Aug. 31
VA Williamsburg, Busch Gardens	Sept. 1
BC Vancouver, World Expo	Sept. 12
WA Puyallup, State Fair	Sept. 13-14
CA Bakersfield, Kern County Fair	Sept. 29
CA Ventura, Fair	Oct. 1

" All dates subject to change "

· Backstage ·

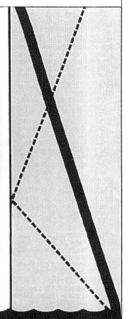

The Beach Boys

Touring: May 30 — December

Artist Management
Concerts West
450 N. Roxbury Dr., 4th Fl.
Beverly Hills, CA 90210

Personal Manager
Tom Hulett

Road Manager/Tour Accountant
Elliot Lott

Booking Agency
William Morris

Agent
Dennis Arfa

The Beach Boys

Lead Vocals
Mike Love

Lead Guitar/Lead Vocals
Carl Wilson

Guitar/Vocals
Alan Jardine

Keyboards/Vocals
Brian Wilson
Bruce Johnston

Back-up Musicians
Guitar/Vocals
Jeff Foskett

Bass
Ed Carter

Keyboards
Billy Hinsche

Keyboards/Synthesizer
Mike Meros

Drums/Percussion
Mike Kowalski
Bobby Figoura

Sound Company
Showco, Dallas

House Soundmixer
Gary Kudrna
Jeff Peters (Ind.)

Stage Monitor Mixer
Chris Kudrna

Lighting Company
Obie's Lighting, Los Angeles

Lighting Designer/Director
John Rossi

Lighting Crew
Don Marshall
Ed McNeil

Bus & Truck Company
Ego Trips, Philadelphia

Truck Drivers
Jerry "Boogie" Nerison
Jim "Mr. Security" Farley

Rigger
Stephen Drown

Production Manager
Matthew Sheppard

Guitar/Keyboard Tech
Ab Jackson

Guitar Tech
Chaz Yost

Drum Tech
Paul Bergerot

Publicity
Rogers & Cowan

Travel Agency
Showstoppers/Sam Contractor, Burbank

Merchandise
Tom Collins Enterprises, Minneapolis

Corporate Sponsor
Sunkist

· The Week In Box Office ·

ZZ Top hangs onto the No. 1 TOPS IN PERFORMANCE spot for the fifth week in a row, and does so with a vengeance. The band shoots way ahead of any other act on the road so far this year in both the attendance and gross categories. As noted on the Top Grossing Acts of the Week chart, ZZ Top has already accumulated close to $10 million in gross and has performed for more than a half million people. These figures, of course, do not include the grosses and attendance numbers from the European portion of their tour earlier this year.

The band's closest competition comes from Loverboy, logging in with a little more than half of ZZ's total gross to date, at $5.8

million and a bit more than 400,000 in attendance. Incidentally, the majority of the U.S. dates reported to *PERFORMANCE* this year for *both* bands have been presented by **Beaver Productions**. Beaver is the only promoter to appear on the new Top Grossing Promoters of the Week chart every week since its inception in the March 7, 1986 issue...

Last week in this space we suggested that our readers keep an eye on **The Firm, Ozzy Osbourne** and **Van Halen**, all of whom had impressive debuts on last week's TOPS chart. Of the three, Ozzy was the only one to make an equally impressive second week jump, moving from No. 27 to 16.

That's not to say, however, that The Firm didn't have an impressive week. On the contrary, the band reports three concerts this week consisting of two sellouts and one 14,625-tickets sold near sellout, moving them upward three spots to No. 11. The Firm was undoubtedly held down on the chart by the momentum of the week's top 10...

As reported here last week, Van Halen's last appearance on the *PERFORMANCE* charts had them jumping straight to No. 5 on their second week on the charts. After a 1986 debut at No. 29 last week the band moozies up to No. 28 since no figures were reported for the band despite an active itinerary... •

SUNKIST cont'd from page 20

Beach Boys carry that strong public identification factor," affirms Prudhomme. "Part of what we're trying to emphasize is brand-identification — and present as much of a proprietary marketing opportunity for Sunkist. The big thing is to find something that's unique, that's readily recognizable — and has a good image. Our involvement with the Beach Boys has given us that uniqueness." Prudhomme indicates finding the right combination is often elusive, adding, "Many brands are trying to do that — and we were presented a unique opportunity to pull it off."

Aside from standardized merchandising of "Beach Boy Clothing," and other items indigenous to the surfing culture, Sunkist plans to introduce a plethora of products to be placed in point of purchase displays in stores around the country, as well as being utilized in promotional giveaway situations. Among the promotional considerations are a sweepstakes-style contest which will allow a lucky pair of attendees the opportunity to ride the wild surf on Hawaii's shore. The trip-tickets are scheduled for presentation during the Beach Boy's finale-concert in December. Prudhomme indicates many tour dates are yet to be firmed up, allowing that many of the coastal appearances may be subject to change.

Concession sales will include merchandise of a "historic" nature, in the form of a photographic text which will offer highlights in a 25-year retrospective of the group's career, in addition to the release of a musical collection. Prudhomme indicates both the text and album will be available to the public as a set, at concerts as well as via mail-in situations. "We're always looking to create excitement for the brand," says Prudhomme, "at both the bottler-level and the consumer level. The Anniversary tour gives us a unique kind of excitement on which to build local promotions, radio merchandising activities and television advertising." Television commercials have been de-

signed in 60- and 30-second formats to be utilized as advance publicity as well as for concert integration. "They're really devised to alert the concert-goers' awareness of the event to take place," says Prudhomme. "We've secured a lot of vintage footage from the Ed Sullivan and Red Skelton shows — and many of their other TV appearances." The clips have been assembled into a nostalgia-montage, incorporating some of the groups more recent concerts. Prudhomme comments, "It kind of brings them into the future with some fancy special effects."

From a budgetary standpoint, he indicates that the video presentation was costly, "but we feel it's money well spent." The campaign was a cooperative situation between Sunkist and MEGA, in the coordination of in-store and broadcast promotions. "They work with promoters at each of the concert-sites to make sure we have a successful tour. It requires a tremendous amount of effort and detail for everybody involved — and MEGA has taken a great burden off of us."

In terms of dollar-generation, Sunkist sees the immediate value in revitalization of their current product as well as upcoming

products. "In dollar terminology, it means share and volume and we want to generate as much of that as we can. We've got some goal and demographic projections out, but there's no fixed number. We're primarily looking at product awareness right now and obviously ending up with some sales volume and sale-share in soft drinks that we can pursue. We've got some pretty optimistic goals for the concert tour if we can pull the promotions off, and we think at this point that it will be pretty successful."

Target cities will include a combination of major metropolitan areas from coast to coast and down the center of the country. Prudhomme speculates that several coastal concerts will be conducted in New York and Los Angeles areas. The campaign will be augmented with an extensive media-merchandising program utilizing radio and television, and mail-in sales. From the individual-city promoter/venue standpoint, the combined efforts will allow more promotional dollars to be spent in touting the tour, allowing each individual show to evolve into an "event." Says Margery Singer, vice president of marketing for MEGA, "This is a joint effort of a major project which affords Sunkist a lot of association with a terrific group – and it's a good match." •

20 Years after — BUDDY HOLLY Hotter than Ever!

THE *Time Barrier* EXPRESS

No. 24
Apr.–May 1979
$1.75

INTO THE ROOTS OF ROCK & ROLL

The
BEACH BOYS
From the Beginning

The Return of
JAN & DEAN

JACKIE WILSON

ROCK & ROLL
Film pix

MARVELOWS

Plus Much More
for the Fan and
Record Collector!

courtesy: Ed Engel

The Beach Boys From the Beginning: An Interview

by Ralph M. Newman & Jeff Tamarkin

While our original intention for these pages was a "conventional" Beach Boys article, those plans suffered an 11th hour abortion when the group suddenly became available for an interview, literally as we went to press. The occasion was a 4 day series of appearances [March 1-4] at New York's Radio City Music Hall, only the first evening of which saw Brian Wilson join the five other members on stage. A more extensive tour is planned for late March and April.

Participating in this question and answer session were Carl Wilson [CW] and Bruce Johnston [BJ]; Dennis Wilson had been scheduled as well, but did not attend. Questions on behalf of TBE were posed by Jeff Tamarkin and Ralph M. Newman — Ed.

TBE — You've been Beach Boys all of your adult lives. If "Surfin' " or "Surfin' Safari" and some of those other early things hadn't happened, if they hadn't been hits, what do you think your direction would have been, what do you think would have happened?
CW — Exactly what did happen.
TBE — You just would have continued on the same course?
CW — What happens, happens.
TBE — It was your intent to continue pursuing this?
CW — Apparently!
BJ — I think that if I had grown up where I was born, in Chicago, I would have wound up in Chicago. Your music is going to come out.
TBE — Yeah, but there are so many

instances of people who started out and the first few things didn't happen, who got frustrated and went back to the car wash, and that was that.
BJ — I think it's all mapped out for you, it's all programmed anyway. I don't fight anything that happens to me, I just let it roll.
TBE — Bruce, when did your paths first cross, you and the Beach Boys?
BJ — I had this funny thing happen, I was about 20 and I was going to Hawaii. I was checking in at the airport and I met their father, in '63 or so. "Well son, I see you have a surf board in your arm, and my sons are playing in Hawaii. They're called The Beach Boys, da da da da." It was great. And I went, and had the best time. I heard them back up Jackie DeShannon, who was doing very complicated songs at that time, and I thougt "Whooaahh, not bad." Then I got to know the guys a little bit. Then Mike called me, cause he knew that I knew people and they needed someone to replace Glen Campbell.
TBE — Had you made the Bruce & Terry records already, at this point?
BJ — Yeah, Not in '63 and '64. We had made a record called "Hey, Little Cobra," that we produced and sang. We started to put our own names on it and nothing happened But it was the whole thing that was happening on the West Coast, a certain kind of music that we were all plugged into.
TBE — Yeah, there were all those studio records — The Four Speeds, etc.;
BJ — Oh, I don't know that group.
TBE — Was Dennis in that group? The

records were released on Challenge.
BJ — You just put it into the super minor leagues there!
CW — I sort of like that Ronnie & The Daytonas record, though. It was pretty cool, right?
BJ — That's a national record. That was great.
TBE — How did you first get involved with Jan & Dean? You all went to high school together?
BJ — They're older than I am, but I skipped a year of school. I went to high school when I was 14, and I think the next year Dean went into the army. But, we knew each other and I lived two blocks from Jan up in Belair. I just used to walk up to his house and use his two-track.
TBE — Was there any truth to the story that you, Jan & Dean, Sandy Nelson and Phil Spector and a bunch of people had a group? What was the name?
BJ — That's right, separately though. Sandy and I used to back Jan and Arnie and Dean. And then Sandy Nelson, Phil Spector and I were all in a band, there was no name. He got us into demos, into making records and told us about Western Recorders. This was '57 and he was just getting into it.
TBE — Were you indeed asked to play piano on "To Know Him Is To Love Him" by The Teddy Bears?
BJ — That's right. I had a date with this girl, and I had a ride. I thought that would be more important.
TBE — Do you still think so? [facetiously]
BJ — Yeah, I wouldn't been able to handle

Dave Patrick

Peter Kanze Collection

On the "Andy Williams Show," 1965.

courtesy: Capitol Records

it, at all. You know when you're 15 years old, have a number one record, even though you'd just be a session musician. In *those* times, that was 20 years ago, that would turn your head around.

CW — Sure would, pretty fast, too.

TBE — **Where you involved with any other of Phil's productions?**

BJ — Not really. I was backing up Ritchie Valens, for a whole summer, when Spector was recording. That was as close as I got.

TBE — **Before we leave the minor leagues altogether, I have to ask you this. Do you remember a record called "Surfer Moon" by Bob & Sheri?**

CW — On Safari? Sure.

TBE — **There were rumors for years, which Brian has since denied, that Brian was "Bob." He says it was someone named Bob Norbert.**

CW — It is Bob Norman, er Bob Norburg

TBE — **Do you know who Sheri is?**

CW — Yeah, she was a girl named Sheri.

TBE — **Do you know her last name?**

BJ — Netherland (laughter) *[Ed. note: The Sherry Netherland is the hotel across the street from where this interview was taking place.]* Her first initial was T.

TBE — **Seriously, folks . . .**

CW — She was this real nice girl, I don't remember her last last name. That was way back.

TBE — **Another question in that vein. There was the record on "X" and the record on Candix, "Surfin." Do you recall why it came out on those two labels?**

CW — I have no idea. I thought it was on Candix. I didn't know about "X". Maybe it was a test pressing or something, I really don't know.

TBE — **There have been reams of material speculating on that stuff. Also, over the years, there were things that appeared on albums and there were different versions on singles.**

CW — . "Help Me Rhonda."

TBE — **Yeah, "Help Me Rhonda," "Be True To Your School." I've noticed that "Be True To Your School" always appears one way on singles and the other way on albums. Is that coincidence or is there some philosophy behind that?**

CW — Sounds like it was an album cut and then got cut for a single.

TBE — **You just went in and cut them over to make them singles?**

BJ — Well, I remember trying to talk Brian into putting the *new* version of "Help Me Rhonda" on the "*Summer Days, Summer Nights*" album. I've been trying to talk Carl into putting the single version of "Here Comes The Night" on the next album, but we probably won't do that. We'll wait till the greatest hits album. I'm being silly, but that's what happens — you cut another version and it becomes a hit sometimes, and you stick it on the next album.

TBE — **Are you aware of how avidly your material is collected? And the value of some of the things that you've done? Do you know that some early records are selling for $500-600 per copy? Like the Bob & Sheri?**

BJ — Which ones? (laughter) What's the highest value? What actual *Beach Boy* record is worth the most?

TBE — **Oh, the highest would be Kenny & The Cadets, original copies.**

CW — I was on that record, I think.

TBE — **Were you really?**

CW — Wasn't it Kenny, my Mom, Brian and me? We went down to this guy's house just for fun you know.

TBE — **Wasn't it Brian, your mother, Al and there was, what was his name — Gary — he wrote a few things on "*Surf's Up*"?**

BJ — Gary Usher?

TBE — **No, Winfrey . . .**

CW — Oh, Winfrey, that's Alan's friend.

TBE — **Does that sound possible?**

CW — Gary Winfrey? I'm not relating to what you're saying.

BJ — What *Beach Boys* records are worth a lot of money?

TBE — **The "X" record is selling for a lot — also the two Candix numbers.**

BJ — I hope you're working your way up to my shrink wrap of "*Pet Sounds*" and "*Smiley Smile*."

CW — It's fun thinking about that. It's wild!

TBE — **There are "*Smile*" covers around that sell for a great deal.**

BJ — They're not the reprints those guys were doing?

TBE — No, these are the originals.

BJ — Well, David Leaf looked at my stuff, 'cause he was researching his book *[The Beach Boys & The California Myth]* and said: "You've easily got about $20,000 worth of Beach Boys stuff sitting in your garage." And, the next day, I moved my stuff to Beacon's (a storage warehouse) and then let him look at my stuff — I thought the guy had walked into the king's treasure chamber! Right in Beacon's! (to Carl) I have a video tape . . . do you remember that video tape we did for Maharishi? We were down South and did a "Hi, this is the Beach Boys for Maharishi . . . we'll see you at Madison Square Garden." (laughter) I have that on a 2-inch.

CW — (to Bruce) I'd love to see it — would that be great.

BJ — Oh, it's great! And I have tapes of us playing at McCormack Place before it burned down, some of them on 2-track, with sound. I would take things as I walked out the door and save everything!

CW — Just a scrapbook, huh? We've got to move into Beacon's for the summer!

BJ — I have boxes *this* high (gestures) filled with stuff. I've got three years of hotel keys and every picture that's ever been printed.

TBE — Did you know that Nick Venet auctioned off some gold albums and other items?

CW — His gold albums? He probably only had one.

TBE — There were several of them floating around.

BJ — I wouldn't put it past him.

CW — That's really bizarre, cause he only did the first record.

TBE — Somehow or another he got his hands on them and they're around.

CW — [facetiously] Brian said "Get 'em outta here;" also, anybody at the label can get them made.

BJ — No not the ones with the brown frames. They don't make presentation . . .

CW — Oh, they don't make those old ones anymore.

BJ — Those are the ones I have.

TBE — There are people who collect graphics — every foreign picture sleeve, every label variation, etc.

BJ — Wow, I have all that!

TBE — What is your reaction to the fact that there are so many people who spend their salaries every week to do this?

CW — I think that's really sweet — I do. I think it's kinda interesting, I think it's something to do. It's a hobby and if they love the music — then that's all right. I think that's great.

TBE — It gets a little weird when people put plastic and paper over music. They start collecting pictures and labels and never play the records.

BJ — They're collecting things that turn 'em on, in happier times probably. Reminders.

TBE — OK . . . How do you like playing Radio City?

CW — I like it. I can't really see the audience too well, though. I'm used to being able to have eye-to-eye contact. It's difficult there, so . . .

TBE — Does the orchestra pit bother you?

CW — Yeah, well, I prefer being right with the audience. I *love* that.

TBE — We were amazed to see how many people you have with you. Could you just briefly run down who was on stage? Were most of the people from Celebration?

courtesy: Ed Engel

CW — No, no, no . . . well, Ed Carter playing bass, he's been with us for a long time. Bobby Figueroa, he's on drums. Phil Shenale is playing synthesizer. I think Overheim is the name of his synthesizer. And . . . (to Bruce) what's Mike's last name?

BJ — Mike Love?

CW — NO! (general laughter) Mike *in the band.*

BJ — Oh, Mike Meros. What a player!

CW — He's playing clavinette and synthesizer stuff . . . he's great.

BJ — We're just using him for these three days. He's teaching the rest of the band "Here Comes The Night," 'cause he played on the record.

TBE — How did the concept of using five keyboard players come about?

CW — We just said, "Hey . . . ." I don't know, it just came up.

BJ — I added one, then I added myself. I think it's too many.

CW — Sterling Smith is playing piano, Carli Munoz is playing organ, and Bruce is playing electric piano.

TBE — Bruce, how did you come back to playing with the band?

BJ — Brian called me and asked me to get involved. And the guys had been talking about it. I kind of decided that if I was going to do the next album it would be a

Suzanne Newman

Carl, right, poses with Bruce & Family (Ozzie and Harriet!),

Suzanne Newman

Bruce (left) and Carl chat with Ralph M. Newman, 3 / 4 / 79, just prior to their Radio City Music Hall performance.

good idea to come on the road. Not on this trip, but when we get rolling . . . maybe go down to Al's room . . .

CW — When you live together it's easier.

BJ — Kind of . . . "Hey Al, what about that song you showed me . . ." You know, just start using up that time. There's a lot of time available on the road that you can make more productive without overworking.

TBE — Did you know at the time that Brian wouldn't be very much involved with this tour?

CW — No, we had no idea at that time. See, Alan and I had been talking with each other and we both said how great it would be for Bruce to come back in, and be involved with us. Dennis had also expressed that on his own, and Brian totally independently, again, had called Bruce and said "Come on down to Miami." Then Bruce, Harriet and Ozzie came down.

BJ — Yeah, my family.

CW — We started recording, and then we did some shows. It was really fun.

BJ — Did you see Brian Thursday night?

TBE — Yeah, That's the only show he played, right?

CW & BJ — Uh huh.

TBE — He just flew in for that one day, and then flew back?

BJ — How "jet-setty." (laughter)

TBE — Getting to the current album — it would appear that Brian is less involved again in the writing and production.

CW — Yeah, to some degree, sure.

BJ — Except that he wrote my two favorite Beach Boys sounding things. He wrote this thing with Carl called "Good Timin," which I think is terrific, and "Here Come The Night." That's Brian and Mike.

CW — And Brian sang on "Angel Come Home" and other background parts.

TBE — It was our understanding that "Good Timin" was recorded some years ago. Is that true or was it done at the same

time as the rest of the album?

CW — We wrote it . . . Brian made it up about three years ago, I think. And then, about a year and a half ago, we were up at Caribou Ranch, up at Jimmy Guercio's place and we did the basic cut there.

BJ — But we sang it in October.

TBE — So the track's been in existence for three years?

CW — No, the track's been in existence for about a year, a year and a half.

TBE — Are there other similar pieces of material, that might surface on future albums?

CW — I don't think so.

TBE — Wasn't there an album that was going to be delivered late in '77?

CW — Yeah, I think that's on the shelf, I don't know.

TBE — You don't think that any of that will see the light of day?

CW — It won't surface with me. I don't have anything to do with it.

TBE — "Here Comes The Night" is a definite shocker, the first time you hear it.

CW — It is a surprise . . . it's a big hello.

TBE — Who's idea was it to cut it in that vein?

CW — Well, it was Bruce's idea.

BJ — My friend Curt Becher, who produced The Millenium and The Association. When I told him I was going to get involved with the guys, he said, "You know that song, "Here Comes The Night," on the "Wild Honey" album?" I said yeah. "Why don't you do that?" And so I went to the guys, and they went for it, They weren't sure of the way we were going to present it, but it just kinda evolved from Curt's idea. As it turned out . . . a lot of the interviews we do, people are reading more things into it then what went down. It just turned out that we had a chance to stretch out vocally. There's, I figure, nine minutes of vocals. Forget the "12-inch." The "12-inch" is a concession we made to disco. We have to cut a verse and

chorus out, slow it down, add some more drums . . . so, that's O.K. and that's working. But the album version was cut that long and it gave us a chance to try, I won't say vocal tricks, but to go through vocal exercises 'cause our thing has been a vocal orientation. We boiled the single version down to a little over four minutes.

TBE — So the album version is different from the 12-inch" and the "7-inch" also?

CW — Oh, yeah.

BJ — The album version is so hot. Well, the "7-inch" is really hot. I really feel like we're going to get some kind of vocal arranging award as a group for that record, or something from somebody. It's really all the stuff we've been trained to do, it just happens to be commercial too. But, I mean, it's something that nobody is going to do, with four-part harmony.

TBE — How would you sum up the role of The Beach Boys in 1979 and in the 1980s? In concert, it's still the oldies that get the most audience response. And the new songs, although they are well received, don't knock them out.

CW — It's a little early in this particular game, with the new album, to say what that is going to be. Naturally they're going to respond to the tunes that are more well known. But after they hear this album, maybe these tunes will become real well known, also.

BJ — You know, when The Bee Gees changed style, they went from (sings) "I've gotta get a message to you" into some new stuff. If they started doing their new stuff on stage and people hadn't heard it, they'd say "OK, but sing (sings) 'How can you mend a broken heart." You know, once anything starts happening on the radio, it's hot . . . it just becomes part of your thing.

TBE — We don't think that The Bee Gees are tied to an "image" as you are, though.

BJ — No.

CW — That seems so. Anyway, I agree.

Beach Boys Ballet Debuts

■ NEW YORK — The Robert Joffrey Ballet Company of New York will perform a new ballet entitled "Deuce Coupe" to fifteen songs recorded by the Beach Boys during their career. The ballet was debuted in Chicago as part of the Joffrey repertory, and will be presented in New York when the company opens there on March 1. Included in the ballet are Beach Boys' songs "Devoted to You," "Feet Pete," "Don't Go Near the Water," "Look at Tomorrow," "Cuddle Up," "Got to Know the Woman," "Deuce Coupe," "Little Honda," "Buga Loo," "Alley Oop," "A-Papa-Oo-Mau-Mau" "Catch a Wave," "Mama Says," and "Wouldn't It Be Nice."

Elton John (piano) and Dennis Dragon (Daryl's brother, second from left) join The Beach Boys on "Good Vibrations From London," a TV special aired 7 / 18 / 72.

Peter Kanze Collection

courtesy: Ed Engel

41

courtesy: Ed Engel

Peter Konze Collection

courtesy: Capitol Records

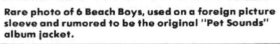

Rare photo of 6 Beach Boys, used on a foreign picture sleeve and rumored to be the original ''Pet Sounds'' album jacket.

courtesy: Capitol Records

The Honeys join The Beach Boys, Hollywood Bowl ''Y'' Day, 11 / 1 / 63; this is the only known stage photo of the 2 groups together.

courtesy: Ed Engel

TBE — Does that still bother you at this point that you are that tied to an image.

CW — No. People can have any image they want. It's uplifting people's spirits, that's all.

TBE — How would you sum up Brian's role, at this point? Is he going to be more involved?

CW — He really enjoys going on the road these days. He had a real rough spell last year, so he stopped traveling again. But he wants to come out with us in April and be more involved. We have twenty dates set for late spring.

TBE — How do you see your audience now? Is it pretty much the same audience? Do you think that the younger kids understand your past? Or are they just relating to what you're doing now?

CW — I don't know how much they know about our past history — the charge is on the music. There are a lot of really young kids and they're singing along. We're in a time warp in some ways, it's really interesting.

TBE — Do you think they're picking up on the new music, though?

CW — Well, we'll see when this album really gets out. But, I think so.

TBE — How much of a role does TM play in your lives these days?

CW — It plays very little part in my life. I became a member of the Movement of Spiritual Inner Awareness, last July. And so, I'm doing a different form of mediation, more accurately called a "Spiritual Exercise."

TBE — How does that differ from TM?

CW — It's perhaps a more active technique of meditation.

TBE — What about the rest of the band?

CW — Michael and Alan are still involved with the TM technique, and I think that's about it.

TBE — We were wondering what you thought of David Leaf's book.

CW — I haven't read it. I've heard about it. My Mom told me after she read it.

TBE — Do you think it conveys the group's history pretty well? Have any of the Beach Boys, other than yourself, expressed satisfaction with it?

CW — Well, I don't know, I heard some complaints. I heard about some things that were inaccurate, but I don't have a lot of energy on that book. It's O.K. with me that it's out. It's all right.

TBE — The transition that you made during the "Pet Sounds" period, was that a very hard period for you?

CW — Yes.

TBE — Does that compare at all with what you're going through now? Putting out "Here Comes The Night" — do you feel that there's a comparison?

CW — I feel that this time there's just a lot more positive. There's just not the negativity that there was at that time and during "Smiley Smile." It was just a real rough time.

TBE — Why was it such a rough time — was it the image that you had?

CW — Oh, it was a lot of things . . . that I suppose was part of it. Brian's involvement with LSD was pretty rough on him.

TBE — If you could compare the southern California scene that you're involved with from the 60s to now, how has it changed? What were some of the major changes?

CW — My life has gone through real big changes, my life is quieter now. My private

life is a lot quieter. It's just a lot more organized just speaking in terms of my own thing.

TBE — What has led to your switch to Caribou and CBS?

CW — The relationship we had with Warner Brothers, I guess for a lot of reasons, never really worked out very well. And we wanted very much to be with CBS and Jim Guercio and CBS wanted very much to be with us. So it was just a thing we both went after. So the lawyers got together and worked it out.

TBE — Is there more artistic freedom involved? Was Warners stunting you at all?

CW — It's more artistic *support*. I don't even know if I like the idea of *so-called* artistic freedom, because I like the feedback. It's good for me. Like when we were recording the album, Bruce would, . . . I would do a vocal and he would respond to it. If it didn't sound right, I never got put off by it or thought (whines) "Well, he thought I was shitty" or something like that. It was feedback and it was a way for me to . . .

BJ — I had to use different ways of diplomacy in this album. Certain people I can say: "EEEggghhh, you can do it better you know . . . , I think that . . . , There's

With Capitol Records execs, accepting platinum records for "Endless Summer," 10/74.

Dave Patrick

The Beach Boys Today! and Tomorrow

by David Leaf

Because much of the accompanying interview focuses on the history of The Beach Boys, it might be appropriate to take somewhat of a closer look at their present status and future directions.

First, it is necessary to remember that in the summer of 1976, The Beach Boys were at the peak of one of the most successful comebacks in rock history. It was centered around the return of Brian Wilson to active, if not totally wholehearted, participation with the group. Less than three years later, The Beach Boys have dissipated almost all of the career momentum generated by 1976's media hype.

Very simply, relatively few people are really interested in The Beach Boys' new records. The old hits continue to move at a brisk rate, especially considering the number of times the same songs have been repackaged. The Beach Boys recent studio efforts, however, haven't been successful. While "15 Big Ones" did go Gold "Love You" and "M.I.U." were commercial failures. Without examining its musical merits, it is significant that a group of The Beach Boys' stature struggled to sell 200,000 (or even 100,000) copies of a new album filled with Brian Wilson songs. What's wrong?

Judging by recent concert grosses, everything is fine. The Beach Boys 1978 tour of Australia and New Zealand was a huge financial success, and their 1978 tours in the U.S. mostly have been as lucrative as their live shows have been since 1974. Interestingly, The Beach Boys are unable to sell new music at a rate anywhere near commensurate with their concert drawing power.

The first problem lies within the records themselves. Two of the group's most recent albums have been an uncomfortable compromise between oldies and often weak attempts to exploit The Beach Boys' own 16-year old formula. On rarer occasions, such as on a song like "The Night Was So Young," Brian Wilson is allowed to expand and expound his musical ideas. Unhappily, the best of those personal songs remain "in the can," locked away out of public hearing. When one hears the songs that have been released, there remains no explanation for the unreleased status of songs like "It's Over Now" and "Still I Dream of It."

The studio indecision that has resulted in a long silence between albums is partly the result of the internal difficulties which constantly threaten to end The Beach Boys. One of the more curious recent developments in Beach Boys' recorded history has been the release of the MCA movie soundtrack, "Almost Summer," with an album cover boasting of the inclusion of music by Brian Wilson, Mike Love, and Al Jardine. The title song, co-authored by

Brian with Al did well as a single, but it was really no more than a pale reflection of songs like "Do It Again" and "It's OK." The new record, however, was not a Beach Boys record. The label said that it was by a group called "Celebration" featuring Mike Love. Mike and his new group, which consists largely of musicians who tour with The Beach Boys, have made numerous free concert appearances in Southern California as well as a guest shot on American Bandstand and the Mike Douglas Show. Brian, brother Carl, and Jan & Dean joined Mike onstage at one show at USC.

Exactly what the formation of Celebration means is unclear at this time. For Mike Love, always the most career conscious of all The Beach Boys, Celebration appears to be a base of operations that is his sole province — a group that could carry on the in-person "good-time" musical tradition of The Beach Boys should they stop touring on a temporary or permanent basis. Considering that recent Beach Boys concerts have provided few "Good Vibrations," a separation might be preferable to the spectacle of these aging Beach Men going through the motions of being Beach Boys. Their current onstage demeanor makes it obvious that they don't enjoy working together. If the music doesn't soon become fun for them, that attitude will eventually

get through to the audiences.

Their last record, "M.I.U." is thankfully a real Beach Boys LP. While the lyrical themes still aren't fully satisfying, they also aren't embarrassing except on a song like "Hey Little Tomboy." What really matters it that they're singing like the Beach Boys for the first time in years. From Brian's wonderful falsetto on "She's Got Rhythm" to the beautiful vocals by Al and Mike on "Winds of Change," the group's singing and harmonies are at a peak not heard since 1970's overlooked classic, "Sunflower." It's a good feeling.

As the group entered the studio last fall for their first album for Caribou, it was with a spirit of teamwork that's been missing for quite a while. The addition of former Beach Boy Bruce Johnston in the studio as well as the guidance and expertise of Chicago's mentor, Jim Guercio, hopefully will give this album a promise that may make this a landmark effort in the group's recorded catalogue.

While work on that disk was underway, Dennis temporarily shelved his solo career; but now that the LP is finished, Dennis' career will receive more attention from him. If Dennis is to make it on his own and have a firm identity as a solo artist, this may be the time to wean himself away from The Beach Boys. A Dennis Wilson tour would go a long way towards establishing his solo career, but personal problems make an artistic commitment from Dennis difficult at the moment. For the other Beach Boys, their future doesn't seem to be as clearly defined as Dennis' or Mike's. With "M.I.U.", Alan Jardine has proved his ability as a producer is worth further attention. Carl and Brian have always had unlimited potential, and it is totally up to them how far they intend to develop their skills. As for the group, they've all been doing this for a long time, and how much longer depends on a number of factors, some of which are financial.

The last two years of the Beach Boys existence has been filled with much public speculation that the group's demise is imminent. Privately, there always appears to be considerable strife, but that isn't unusual for this is a group that knows trouble intimately. Recently, a new calm descended upon the group. The Beach Boys have survived as a band for over sixteen years, and there is no concrete indication that things will change in the near future. In fact, for the first time since the early 70s, the group seems to be determined to create new music worthy of their past triumphs. The singing on the "M.I.U." album is solid evidence that they can all do it when they try. Their next album on Caribou will be the one to watch for. In the meanwhile, "M.I.U." is their most listenable effort since "Surf's Up" in 1971.

For the Beach Boys, who themselves rarely know what tomorrow will bring, nothing will be a surprise. And that includes the possible release of outtake versions of the legendary "Fire" tapes.

David Leaf is the author of The Beach Boys and the California Myth *[Grosset & Dunlap], a new book containing hundreds of rare and unpublished photos as well as the most definitive account of Brian Wilson's life and* The Beach Boys' *career ever published. Leaf also published and edited the temporarily-defunct* Pet Sounds *magazine, and is the co-author of* The Illustrated Bee Gees, *their authorized biography. It will be co-published this year by Delilah Communications and Dell.* ◉

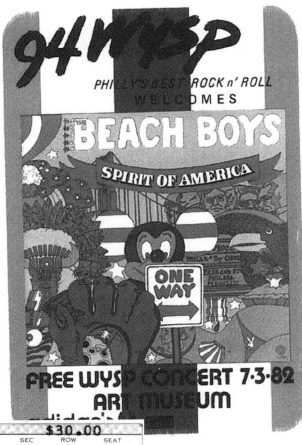

Trouser Press

Jan./Feb. 1981
Vol. 3, No. 3
$1.00
UK 50p

Collectors' Magazine

Ex-Beach Boy
Interviewed,
page 1

A Bonzo Baedeker, page 6

Promo Records, page 8

A BEACH BOY LOOKS BACK: Boyish, Boy Good, Clean Fun

Brian, Mike, Dennis and Carl Wilson, with David Marks at far right. 'I was just their kid friend going, "Hey guys, can I play too?"'

By Robert DuPree

Stardom. Screaming fans. A string of hit singles rocketing to the top of the national charts. Making it while you're young enough to enjoy the megabucks and international recognition that stardom brings. It's the fantasy that makes the music business what it is, making some of us musicians, and many more fans. It's the star trip, and tickets to ride come few and far between.

But for David Lee Marks, the fantasy became real. At age 12, when most people are riding their bikes and pondering puberty, David Marks was a bona fide star, a founding member of the group still referred to as the American Beatles: the Beach Boys.

Now 32 and recently relocated to Portland, Oregon, Marks consented to lift a 15-year veil of silence and talk about what it was like.

RD: How did you first become involved with the Wilsons?
DM: My family moved to California from Pennsylvania when I was about seven; wanted to see movie stars, I guess. We first lived in a motel across the street from MGM. When I was eight we moved into a house across the street from the Wilson family.
RD: This was in Hawthorne?
DM: Our street was the border between Inglewood and Hawthorne, so there were kid feuds, territorial things. Carl and Dennis were across the street, throwing trash over, that kind of thing.
RD: So you all grew up together?
DM: Right. Dennis and I got really tight and did all sorts of creepy kid things together. There was a long drainage ditch with a quarter-mile of dead grass in it that we set on fire with alcohol from my chemistry set, then watched three companies of firemen race over to put it out. We chopped trees

down in the park, then lied our way out of it when the cops came to our houses. Everyday stuff, y'know.
RD: Good, clean boyish fun.
DM: Sure. Murray, their Dad, ran a machine shop and had a few bucks, so he was always buying them go-carts, spoiling them. I would be over there, playing with their go-carts and telescopes, hanging out. Dennis was a real bully then, punching kids in the mouth, and I was always glad to be on his side.
RD: There was music in the family too.
DM: Right, family sing-a-longs. Mom, Dad, the three brothers and their cousin would get together and sing church-choir songs. They had a piano and Hammond organ in their den, got together to sing.
RD: How did your interest in music develop?
DM: My grandmother bought me a trumpet when I was in fifth grade and I played in the school band. I loved Harry James—saw him on the *Tonight* show or something—and he was who I wanted to be. So I wanted to be a musician early. Then, I saw a guy and his sister, John and Judy Moss, singing with a trio behind them. John had played with Richie Valens. When I saw this guy playing guitar and singing I said to myself, "That's what I want to do." When I was 11, I got a guitar for Christmas and took a few lessons from John. Meanwhile, Carl had taken up guitar in high school and sat in with John's band for a few bar gigs, so he and I started doing Ventures tunes—sitting around the living room, learning them off the records for our own amusement.
RD: What was Brian doing then?
DM: Brian was going to El Camino Junior College, studying music. He was 18 and really into Chuck Berry and the Four Freshmen. He used to really study the Four Freshmen, their harmony. He and his cousin Mike, plus Al Jardin from the junior college and another guy I forget, had a little group, Kenny and the Kadets. They weren't into surf music, they just played for parties and bar mitzvahs and stuff.
RD: So there you were, all practicing together.

DM: Yeah, learning to play guitar. Brian and Carl were on separate trips at the time. Brian with his group, Carl jamming with me and with another guy up the street who had an accordion. But then Brian started taking advantage of the family situation—he *was* the big brother, right?—and began to incorporate us all into his group. "Hey, Carl, why don't you come over here and play this guitar part? I just made up this lick on the piano." Dennis didn't play an instrument but started learning drums. I wasn't really in the group then, though. I was practicing with them, but Al Jardin was playing upright bass with them. I was just their kid friend from across the street, going, "Hey guys, can I play too? Can I, huh, huh?"
RD: So when did the recording career start?
DM: Murray was a failed songwriter. He'd placed a song with Lawrence Welk, but not much else. He had a few contacts in the business. So he told the group, "Hey, why don't you guys record?" He knew a guy with a studio, Candix Records, and the band went down and recorded "Surfin'." I'd been practicing with them, and when they snuck out that record without me, I was really *crushed.*
RD: That was Al playing on the first single?
DM: Yeah. But then Al said, "Well, this is going nowhere," and split to go back to dentistry school.
RD: And so a new star was born.
DM: Right. I was 12 years old, sitting at home with Mommy and Daddy, watching TV and getting ready for school the next day. The Wilsons came over and said, "Do you want to be in the group? We have something going on here." They'd been gigging around town, doing crummy gigs. We all begged my Mom and Dad to let me join. "Aw, gee, can I? Huh, huh?" They finally said yeah, and then sat down to get all the details about money and everything. I couldn't have cared less about money. I just rode around on my bike wishing I could be in the group, y'know? My first gig with them was at the Bel Aire Bay Club, and we wore *ugly* mustard-colored coats that were way too big for us. Es-

1

49

pecially mine. Real nerdy.

RD: Was the group called the Beach Boys in those early days?

DM: No, it was called The Pendletones, which Brian thought would be a real cool name since all the surfers wore Pendleton shirts. "Surfin'" was a local hit in LA and Capitol got interested. An independent promotion man working with us, Russ Reagan, came up with the name "Beach Boys" and we all went, "Yuck!" We all thought it was really embarrassing. But Capitol loved the name, loved the idea, so we stuck with it.

RD: So with a new name and a national label the group was on its way?

DM: Yeah. Capitol leased the master from Candix and released the first single, "Surfin' Safari." This was '62.

RD: And that was your first national hit.

DM: I remember eating dinner one night with my folks, and the song came on the radio. That was a surprise; the next week it was number one. When we picked up a copy of *Billboard*, it was breaking in real strong. Then a couple of weeks went by, and it *just shot* to number one! We were *real* surprised! We didn't plan it, we didn't try to be famous. It was all Murray's doing. We were doing the music, but he promoted it. He had bucks, and that's how he paid off people to play our records.

RD: That's how it was done in those early days—grease the wheels a little.

DM: Yeah, he did a lot of that. And I'm glad he did. If it hadn't been for Murray's business acumen, the group never would've happened. I think he was a genius.

RD: That first single was a double-sided hit. "Surfin' Safari" hit in August, then the flip, "409," hit in October.

DM: Right. I remember we had this guy named Gary Usher with a '59 Chevy, big engine, rear up, going up and down the street, recording that stupid car noise that starts off the record—really pissed off the neighbors. Gary later became an executive with RCA, then got fired.

RD: Did you have any say in those early records, musically?

DM: I had no say in the music at all. It was always Brian. Oh, maybe Mike helped with the lyrics and some of the vocal arrangements, but we were essentially a vehicle for Brian's expression. He'd get us in the den and teach us our guitar parts.

RD: Did the rest of the group resent Brian?

DM: Brian didn't become a dictator. We begged him to take control.

RD: So you were Brian Wilson fans too?

DM: We were his *biggest* fans. When he sat down at the piano and played "Surfin' Safari," and said this is our next hit, I got chills. Got goosebumps, man. We jumped around and pounded him on the back. "God, you're a genius, man!"

RD: So he did everything, even in the studio, from the first.

DM: Complete control, from the word go. His Dad tried to horn in on the producing and Brian would get pissed off,

sound changed a lot. It was smoother and flatter—we started sounding like the Johnny Mann Singers.

RD: The whole group was involved from "Surfin' Safari" on?

DM: Well, Carl, Brian, and Mike always did *all* the singing. Dennis sang a little onstage, but not on the records, at least while I was with them. Y'know, I've actually played on more of those first songs than Dennis did. Brian was really into hiring studio drummers—Hal Blaine and those guys. Dennis had just learned to play drums for the group and was just picking them up. He was a good showman onstage, though.

RD: Let's talk about touring.

DM: It was a *lot* different than it is now. These days, you just get on your plane and show up at the gig. Everything's taken care of, all your stuff is set up, you just do one set. We'd get off the plane, rent a Hertz car and a U-Haul van, and drive from city to city, some of them 700 miles apart. We didn't have roadies; we carried our own amps and suitcases. We had a road manager who stood at the door and counted tickets, because we got half the take plus a straight salary.

RD: Quite a grind for a bunch of kids.

DM: We played four-hour gigs, a lot of dances and things. Then we'd pack up and drive 500 miles to the next city, where we'd sleep in a motel all day until the next night's gig. Just one-nighters, one after another. We were *famous*, the number-one group in the country; and there we'd be playing one-lane bowling alleys and outdoor fairs in Pennsylvania, in the rain, getting shocked by our instruments. We'd get the bends, playing a bowling alley one night and the *Ed Sullivan Show* the next.

RD: You were just 12, 13 years old. How could you handle all that?

DM: It was hard. Out of two or three months touring, there would be maybe two or three days off. I used to get sick backstage. I wasn't drinking or taking dope then but I'd get sick anyway, from the hours, not eating right. I was a trooper. We *had* to do it. There was a lot at stake.

RD: Did Murray set up the tours?

DM: The William Morris Agency—Marshall Berle, Milton Berle's nephew, was our agent. Usually we'd be following somebody from city to city, like the Everly Brothers, who were terrors. They'd be somewhere the night before, leave the place in shambles, destroy the motel—and when *we* got there the city council would be waiting for us: "Behave yourselves, or leave right now!" We had to be careful. We did our share of destroying motels, though. We'd get home from a tour and there'd be a $700 bill waiting for us for a room we'd had a water fight in.

RD: More good, clean boyish fun.

DM: Oh, it was a perfect opportunity to be rowdy and we took full advantage of it. Dennis painted his cock green once,

us to whorehouses.

RD: Whorehouses? How old were you?

DM: I was 14. See, Murray used to go on tours with us, and so did my Dad sometimes, but finally Murray hired this guy named John Hamilton, who had been with the Ventures. He was an old guy, but basically just a rowdy kid. He was one of us, we really loved him. Anyway, this was in Des Moines. We got off the plane and got into a taxi, and Dennis and Mike kept nudging Hamilton. "C'mon, let's get some whores, man!" So the can driver took us to this sleazy hotel with black chicks, sleazy blondes.

RD: You were just 14.

DM: Yeah, she was my first. Carl's first, too. She was washing me off, saying, "Don't come in the pan, kid." I was scared shitless. I wasn't into that, y'know, but I had to go through with it, to be a man, right? "Aw, I ain't chicken!" But I was shaking in my boots. It happened again on my fifteenth birthday too. We were playing an amusement park in Wheeling, West Virginia, owned by a multimillionaire named Walter Dyke. After a show, he took us to a club, a former speakeasy, and—after I had mentioned it was my birthday—Dyke was buying me all the Scotch I could drink, though he knew I was just 15. So he pointed over to this girl sitting in a chair and says, "Ask her to go upstairs with you, and tell her I said it was OK with me." She was about 20, I guess. This was his birthday gift to me. Nice guy. I was too shy to do it, so Dennis bounced over and dragged her upstairs, taking advantage of the situation. Then he came back and said, "I warmed her up for you, go ahead. It's your birthday!" So I went up, and she was on the bed, reading a newspaper, still had her high heels on. "Let me know when you're through, kid." Scared the hell out of me. Boy, were my folks pissed off.

RD: How long did Hamilton last?

DM: Well, Murray flew out to a tour date and saw us carrying on. Fired him on the spot.

RD: When did Al Jardin re-enter the picture?

DM: About a year or so after we started touring. After a-while, Brian got sick of the tour grind. He just wanted to stay home with his girlfriend. So he did the TV gigs and local appearances, but mainly stayed home to produce records and write songs. Al came back to do the road gigs and sing Brian's part onstage but he wasn't on the records while I was with them.

RD: Which albums are you on?

DM: I played on the first five albums and about seven singles, some of them double-sided hits: "Surfin' Safari," "409," "Ten Little Indians," "Surfin' U.S.A.," "Shut Down," "Surfer Girl," "Little Deuce Coupe," "Be True to Your School," "In My Room." "Fun, Fun, Fun" was the first single they did without me. Brian came over to play it on my stereo, to see if it would sound good on the radio.

RD: How did the split happen?

storm out of the studio.

RD: There was friction there.

DM: Murray tried to take all the credit. Brian would get all the settings on the board and go out into the studio, and Murray would change everything. Then Brian would come back in and go, "What the fuck happened? It sounds *different!*" They were fighting all the time.

RD: Why were they so competitive?

DM: I guess Murray was trying to live through his sons. It was finally agreed that Murray wouldn't try to produce any more. Brian did everything. Played, did the arrangements, screwed up the lead sheets himself—he didn't need any help to do that.

RD: Why do you think it worked so well?

DM: You listen to those first albums today and they sound campy, corny—but Brian was dead serious. Like the "Cuckoo Clock Song," "Chug-A-Lug," "Ten Little Indians"—he was dead serious about them all and that's what made them work. It wasn't like Brian was trying to put something over. "Is this commercial? How are we gonna trick these turkeys into buying this?" There was no formulating, no plotting or planning. He was just doing what he loved. He told me he wrote about things that turned him on—girls, cars, high school. It's hard to believe that anyone could be that naive and honest, but he was. That's what made those records successful. You can *feel* the sincerity on them.

RD: Murray was out of his way, but what happened when you signed with Capitol?

DM: Nick Venet at Capitol tried to do the same thing Murray had tried to do: He'd sit back and say, "Yeah, this sounds good, guys. Let's take five for hamburgers." Then he'd put his name on the album as producer.

RD: What were recording techniques and facilities like in '62?

DM: Pretty shabby. Four-track had just come out; limiters had just been invented. We recorded the Candix stuff at Western United Recorders on Sunset Boulevard, a little radio soundstage was used for radio shows. There was a little studio in the back, Studio Three, where we did all our stuff. Western told it like it was—real funky-sounding. The sound, the success of the group, came out of that dinky little studio.

RD: How sophisticated were you? Was everything recorded live, or did you break it up, build it?

DM: We rehearsed at home and did all the instrumental tracks live in the studio. Then Brian, Carl, and Mike overdubbed vocals—two vocal overdubs and that was it. When we started recording for Capitol and using their studios, the

and went down to the lobby naked for a Coke. And we got crab lice once. We were at a music store, standing behind a table, signing autographs. All these little teenage girls were there, and here are these five guys going *[jumps around, scratching crotch vigorously]*. Brian said, "Yep, we got 'em." So we go back to the hotel and put blue ointment on our broken skin. It would burn, and there'd be five guys jumping up and down naked in front of the air-conditioner. Must've looked funny from the street.

RD: How did your friends at school react to your success?

DM: That was the hardest part. All our buddies turned against us. It was hard for them to relate to someone who became famous overnight. They would constantly be on our asses, making fun of us. Fights, constant threats. I'd get cornered and punched in the stomach a lot at school. I realized I wasn't one of them anymore.

RD: How did the surfers react?

DM: The surfers in LA were a gang and they resented the Beach Boys because surfing was a sacred sport to them, they were reverent about it. And they knew we were lying, that none of us ever surfed, even entered the water. Dick Dale and his Deltones were the official surfer band, the surfers adopted him. He actually invented the "surf sound." He had these big fat strings on his guitar, and played through a reverb unit and big Fender amps, though he didn't have our vocal thing going. He was the first to sing "Sloop John B." And we copped his sound, so the surfers hated us. They would go after us in the parking lot after gigs, try to kick our butts good.

RD: So you weren't exactly home-town heroes.

DM: Strangely enough, our records sold real well in LA, too, but it wasn't quite like going back east or to the midwest, where they just worshipped us. I had to quit public school. Carl and I were the only ones left in school at this point. We went to Hollywood Professional School with the movie stars' kids. Kids like Peggy [*Mod Squad*] Lipton, Sue [*Lolita*] Lyons. Dennis was 16, so he could quit altogether.

RD: What did your parents think about all the touring, quitting school? You were just a kid.

DM: They gave up. Oh, at first they were like hawks, but after all that money started rolling in, it was "See you when you get back from the tour, son." There wasn't much else they could do, so they gave up.

RD: The touring must have created havoc with your social life. Did you have a steady girlfriend?

DM: Not really. Our road manager used to take

DM: Well, people assume I was kicked out, because it would be stupid to quit that kind of scene, right? But that's actually what happened.

RD: You quit the group?

DM: See, you've got to remember that we were kids, and we were cocky. It was a little scary, but great, too, playing guitar and getting pressed up against chain-link fences by thousands of teenage girls. So at that young and tender age, I had gotten arrogant. I was a star, right? Five number one hits in a row, and I thought I had it made. So I started getting real cocky. We always had to carry our amps and suitcases, and I started refusing to carry mine. Murray would yell at me, but I didn't care. I didn't have any plans to quit, but Murray started pressuring me because he wanted all the money to be in the corporate family situation, and I made that difficult. My parents and Murray started having conflicts over money, which I really didn't give a shit about.

RD: How did he start pressuring you?

DM: Oh, real funny stuff. Remember the famous surfboard picture? Well, I was on the end, right? Murray used to tear off my picture and hand it to me. He did that a lot. And there were ads and promo things—they'd put Carl's face over mine, so there would be *two* Carls in the picture. Stuff like that.

RD: So when did it happen?

DM: I was with them about three-and-a-half, four years, so I was almost 16. We were in a car on the way to Chicago when I announced I was quitting the group. Murray went, "Well, all right man! Does everybody hear that?" And all the guys went, "Aw, that's bullshit!" It turned out I still had seven months' worth of contracts, so I could've stayed after that if I hadn't started pushing it. I started singing "She's real fine, my 69" and "Little Douche Kit" onstage, and Murray would fine me. He'd fine me for not smiling onstage too. Finally it ended. Just more or less a mutual agreement between Murray and me.

RD: How'd the boys take it?

DM: I don't think the guys were too happy about it, because we'd grown up together and were pretty tight. And I think Brian probably didn't want me to quit because he thought maybe he'd have to go back out on the road or something. But Al took over rhythm guitar and they went on.

RD: Any regrets?

DM: No, not really. I've gotten royalty checks every six months from the group, so I've never had a job, never had to learn a trade. I guess you could say my career is just waiting for checks.

RD: What kind of money are we talking about here?

DM: After I left the group I had $22,000 in a trust fund my folks had set up for me; then during the '60s I'd get $7,000 to $8,000 every six months. Though that wasn't all the money I deserved, since Murray was skimming through various loopholes. I intervened in a lawsuit the Beach Boys had going back in '71, when they were suing Capitol for back royalties, and I got about $30,000 and a better royalty contract. Then, when the first Beach Boys compilation album, **Endless Summer**, came out in '74, I got another $30,000, and six months later, $17,000.

RD: Not bad for three-and-a-half years' work. Did financial security affect your ambitions?

DM: No. After the split, I wasn't sure what to do, so I saw a buddy I'd met through Carl, a drummer who was fooling around with a garage band at Hawthorne High. I walked in and said, "All right, guys, I'm taking over! Gonna make you *stars!*" So we became Dave and the Marksmen, the first rock band to be signed to A&M. We recorded, went on tours of California, got airplay on all the local stations, met a lot of boss jocks—and didn't sell any records. After a year it folded and I found myself taking a lot of LSD and laying on my back in Venice, California. But I was still ambitious. By the time I was 18, I decided it was time to take the guitar seriously, actually learn to play.

RD: And did you?

DM: Yeah, I became pretty good. Hung out in L.A., doing session work with people like Delaney and Bonnie, various ex-New Christy Minstrels, people like that. Then I got *real* serious and decided to go to school up in Boston.

RD: Berklee?

DM: Yeah, for about six months. Then I went to the Boston Conservatory to study classical music, arranging and orchestration with their resident composer. I wrote symphonies, cut off all my hair, wore a trenchcoat, carried a briefcase—a serious music student. That went on for about a year before I said to hell with it and went back to LA to play rock 'n' roll again. I got hooked up there with Buzz Clifford, got into blues and jazz, made some albums with him and some others that never made it, spent some time up in Tulsa with Leon Russell at Shelter—finally became an obscure blues musician. And very good on my instrument. So now I'm up here with Buzz, who moved here a couple of years ago, to get something good going, do some recording.

RD: Do you have any interest in doing a '60s-revival number?

DM: Well, those are my roots, so that'll be of some benefit. People are taking a step backwards because the music then was *better* than it is now. New wave is just old rock 'n' roll, and the kids all think it's new music. Elvis Costello, the Cars, the Knack, they're all

From top: Brian, Carl, Dennis, David, Mike

new groups doing old stuff with a modern flavor. It's definitely the music of the '80s.

RD: How about true revivalists, like Jan and Dean?

DM: I think they're a little late. There's still a lot of nostalgia, though. I'll tell you something funny about Jan and Dean. They used to think the Beach Boys were copying their sound.

RD: Most people feel it was vice-versa.

DM: Well, Jan and Arnie had a hit back in '59 with a song called "Jenny Lee." So, when "Surfin'" came out, and they heard Mike going [*basso*] "Bom-ba-bompa-bom" and Brian going [*falsetto*] "whoo-ee-ooh," they said, "Hey, these guys are copying our sound!" Jan had met Dean by then, in college, so they started hanging arounf and doing surf songs *exactly* like the Beach Boys. We used to hang out together, go on tour. One time a pilot threatened to pull a plane over in Fresno and kick Jan off 'cause he was goofing around so much, screaming, scaring old ladies. The pilot came back and yelled, "I'll land this sonofabitch right in a field if you don't settle down!"

RD: How did Jan react to that?

DM: Jan was funny. He said, "Don't you know me? I'm Jan and Dean!" Nah, I'm glad they're still touring, and that Jan made it back from Dead Man's Curve.

RD: Why have you been so quiet all these years? We were beginning to think of you as the American Pete Best.

DM: I've been embarrassed by it for the last 20 years. No one I know likes the Beach Boys; they haven't progressed musically. Carl can't play the guitar any better today than he did 15 years ago.

RD: You shouldn't be embarrassed. You were the American Beatles.

DM: Yeah, but the Beatles were actually pretty good musicians onstage, though it was hard to hear because of the screaming girls. We had the screaming girls, too, and they covered us up—which was probably fortunate. Our musicianship was never too hot. I think the Beach Boys' musicianship still leaves a lot to be desired.

RD: Were you embarrassed about the money?

DM: Guilty and embarrassed. "Why should I be getting all this money just for having fun? I don't deserve this!" I'd just give it away, blow it.

RD: Hell, you earned that money, David.

DM: I've changed my attitude these days. I *know* now that I deserve that money. Hell, I should've been in the dirt, playing with toy cars, not our getting drunk and fucking whores and doing one-nighters. Now that I'm older I look back and realize that I didn't get to finish school, didn't have any family life. So I do deserve it.

RD: It's just what happened to one person's life.

DM: Right. It wasn't planned at all, just a chance thing. I lived across the street from these guys and we formed a group, never expecting it to be successful. When we became number one in the nation, we were as surprised as anyone. We were just making our music.

RD: So, ultimately, David Lee Marks has no regrets.

DM: No. Carl used to tell me, "If anyone gives you shit, just tell them you're laughing all the way to the bank [*laughter*]." □

Portions of this interview previously appeared in Two Louies, *Portland, Oregon.*

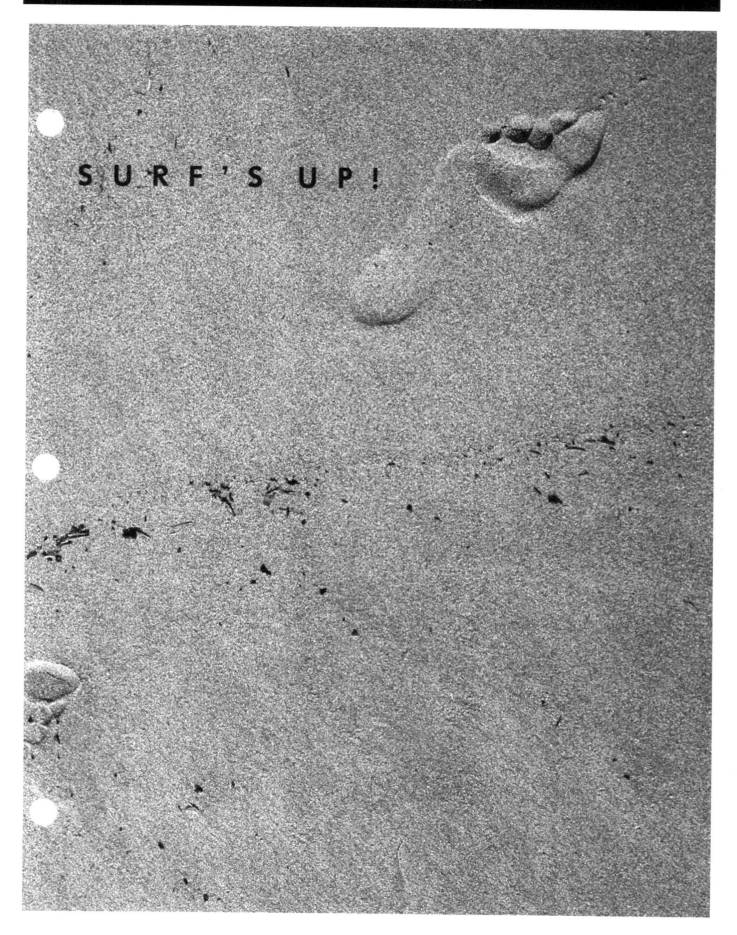

S U R F ' S   U P !

the **BEACH BOYS**

"What's kept me going is the same thing that got me to write 'Surfin'' all those years ago. I wanted to write joyful music that made other people feel good. Music that helps and heals, because I believe that music is God's voice."

BRIAN WILSON,
at the induction ceremony of The Beach Boys into the Rock and Roll Hall of Fame, January, 1988

No Beach Boys record expressed Brian's belief more eloquently than their 1966 masterpiece, Pet Sounds, an album that has not only musically stood the test of time better than perhaps any other sixties release but has become one of the true milestones of rock's most creative era.

The Beach Boys catalog, and especially Pet Sounds have been some of the most eagerly anticipated CD releases since the CD was first introduced. The compact disc reissue series of the vast musical heritage that is the Beach Boys Capitol catalog is kicked off with the coupling of the group's first two LP releases, Surfin' Safari/Surfin' USA, and follow-up releases Surfer Girl/Shut Down Vol. 2. Virtually the entire catalog will follow in the same double-play format and all the wonderful music will be presented in sparkling digitally remastered sound from original

master tapes for your primest listening enjoyment. To spice the deal, each package will offer rare photos from the files and several bonus tracks. These will include 45 mixes (differing from the LP versions) and hard-to-find non-LP B-sides. The icing on the spice is even nicer. Previously unreleased musical curios and gems will appear for the first time. The deepest reaches of the Beach Boys tape vault are now no more remote than the control of your hi-fi.

Keep on reading for additional info on these releases.

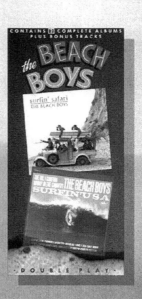

BEACH BOYS
PET SOUNDS

LIST PRICE $9.14
FULL PRICE CD

STREET DATE: 5/15/90
7% OFF INVOICE CD. EXTRA
30 DAYS DATING.
APRIL 9–MAY 18, 1990
C2-48421

- *Pet Sounds* was considered to be one of the most influential records of its time and is still considered a landmark album.
- Contains extended liner notes previously unpublished photos and track-by-track annotation. (Take number, highest chart position)
- Also enclosed is a special interview with Paul McCartney on his thoughts about *Pet Sounds*.
- The entire *Pet Sounds* album is presented in mono as it was originally recorded.
- Contains 3 bonus tracks: "Hang On To Your Ego" and "Unreleased Background" (not currently available) and "Trombone Dixie" (which has never been released before).

TRACKS: WOULDN'T IT BE NICE; YOU STILL BELIEVE IN ME; THAT'S NOT ME; DON'T TALK (PUT YOUR HEAD ON MY SHOULDER); I'M WAITING FOR THE DAY; LET'S GO AWAY FOR AWHILE; SLOOP JOHN B; GOD ONLY KNOWS; I KNOW THERE'S AN ANSWER; HERE TODAY; I JUST WASN'T MADE FOR THESE TIMES; PET SOUNDS; CAROLINE, NO; HANG ON TO YOUR EGO*; UNRELEASED BACKGROUND*; TROMBONE DIXIE*.

BEACH BOYS
SURFIN' SAFARI/SURFIN' USA

LIST PRICE $10.24
FULL PRICE CD

STREET DATE: 5/15/90
7% OFF INVOICE CD. EXTRA
30 DAYS DATING.
APRIL 9–MAY 18, 1990
C2-93691

- Combines the first two Beach Boys releases on Capitol Records.
- Both covers are displayed on the long box and in the CD booklets.
- 24-page CD booklet contains extended liner notes, 4-color album art and previously unreleased photos.
- CD booklet contains detailed track-by-track annotation.
- Contains 3 bonus tracks: "Cindy O Cindy" and "The Baker Man" (never previously released) and "Land Ahoy" (not currently available).

TRACKS: SURFIN' SAFARI; COUNTY FAIR; TEN LITTLE INDIANS; CHUG-A-LUG; LITTLE GIRL (YOU'RE MY MISS AMERICA); 409; SURFIN'; HEADS YOU WIN, TAILS I LOSE; SUMMERTIME BLUES; CUCKOO CLOCK; MOON DAWG; THE SHIFT; SURFIN' USA; FARMER'S DAUGHTER; MISIRLOU; STOKED; LONELY SEA; SHUT DOWN; NOBLE SURFER; HONKY TONK; LANA; SURF JAM; LET'S GO TRIPPIN'; FINDERS KEEPERS; CINDY O CINDY*; THE BAKER MAN*; LAND AHOY*.

BEACH BOYS
SURFER GIRL/SHUT DOWN
VOLUME 2

LIST PRICE $10.24
FULL PRICE CD

STREET DATE: 5/15/90
7% OFF INVOICE CD. EXTRA
30 DAYS DATING.
APRIL 9–MAY 18, 1990
C2-93692

- Both covers are displayed on long box and in the CD booklet.
- Contains extended liner notes, previously unpublished photos and complete track-by-track annotation.
- CD booklet contains detailed track-by-track annotation (take number, highest chart position).
- Contains 3 bonus tracks: "Fun, Fun, Fun" (single version); "In My Room" (German version) and "I Do" (previously unreleased).

TRACKS: SURFER GIRL; CATCH A WAVE; THE SURFER MOON; SOUTH BAY SURFER; THE ROCKING SURFER; LITTLE DEUCE COUPE; IN MY ROOM; HAWAII; SURFERS RULE; OUR CAR CLUB; YOUR SUMMER DREAM; BOOGIE WOODIE; FUN, FUN, FUN; DON'T WORRY BABY; IN THE PARKIN' LOT; "CASSIUS" LOVE VS. "SONNY" WILSON; THE WARMTH OF THE SUN; THIS CAR OF MINE; WHY DO FOOLS FALL IN LOVE; POM POM PLAY GIRL; KEEP AN EYE ON SUMMER; SHUT DOWN, PART II; LOUIE LOUIE; DENNY'S DRUMS; FUN, FUN, FUN (SINGLE VERSION)*; IN MY ROOM (GERMAN)*; I DO*.

*BONUS TRACKS

ADVERTISING
Consumer
Rolling Stone—1/2 page 4-color
Goldmine—full page BW
Co-op
Look for key co-op advertising to be placed around release date.

PRINTED IN U.S.A.

PRESS
All key press across the country will be sent advance copies in an effort to secure major exposure just after the in-store date. The Beach Boys themselves will be working very hard to support these releases.

P.O.P.
- Advance streamers
- Header cards

CHECK STOCK ON:
BEST OF THE BEACH BOYS 91318
CALIFORNIA GIRLS 48046
MADE IN USA 46324
ENDLESS SUMMER 46467

©1990 CAPITOL RECORDS, INC.

The Beach Boys "Double Play" series continues with these latest releases. As with Pet Sounds and the previous two double packs both of these releases contain:

- Original cover art (both covers) displayed on CD long box and in CD booklet.
- 24 page CD booklet with extended liner notes, previously unreleased photos, track by track annotation.
- Bonus tracks—most currently unavailable.
- All tracks were digitally remastered from original master recordings to achieve exceptional sound quality.

BEACH BOYS
LITTLE DEUCE COUPE/
ALL SUMMER LONG

C21Z-93693
FULL PRICE CD

STREET DATE: 6/12/90
7% OFF INVOICE CD. EXTRA
MAY 7–JUNE 15, 1990
C2-93693

- The Beach Boys took the best automotive related blasts already cut for previous discs, ("Little Deuce Coupe," "Shut Down," "Our Car Club," "409") recorded a batch of new ones and put together a concept album dedicated to cars—and Little Deuce Coupe was born.
- *Little Deuce Coupe,* their fourth album, was to become one of the best selling Beach Boys albums ever.
- *All Summer Long* was the 2nd LP of 1964 and their 6th LP release.
- *All Summer Long* was the last studio LP the Beach Boys recorded before Brian Wilson quit the touring band.
- *All Summer Long* represented the first of three Top 10 albums the group would release in 1964 (Concert and Christmas Album would follow) and yielded their first #1 single "I Get Around."
- Bonus Tracks include: "Be True To Your School" (LP version), "All Dressed Up For School" (previously unreleased), "Little Honda" (alternative version), "Don't Back Down" (previously unreleased).

TRACKS: LITTLE DEUCE COUPE; BALLAD OF OLE' BETSY; BE TRUE TO YOUR SCHOOL; CAR CRAZY CUTIE; CHERRY, CHERRY COUPE; 409; SHUT DOWN; SPIRIT OF AMERICA; OUR CAR CLUB; NO-GO SHOWBOAT; A YOUNG MAN IS GONE; CUSTOM MACHINE; I GET AROUND; ALL SUMMER LONG; HUSHABYE; LITTLE HONDA; WE'LL RUN AWAY; CAR'S BIG CHANCE; WENDY; DO YOU REMEMBER?; GIRLS ON THE BEACH; DRIVE-IN; OUR FAVORITE RECORDING SESSIONS; DON'T BACK DOWN; BE TRUE TO YOUR SCHOOL (SINGLE VERSION)*; ALL DRESSED UP FOR SCHOOL*; LITTLE HONDA (ALTERNATE TAKE)* DON'T BACK DOWN (ALTERNATE TAKE)*

*BONUS TRACKS

BEACH BOYS
TODAY/SUMMER DAYS AND
SUMMER NIGHTS

C21Z-93694
FULL PRICE CD

STREET DATE: 6/12/90
7% OFF INVOICE CD. EXTRA
30 DAYS DATING.
MAY 7–JUNE 15, 1990
C2-93694

- The Beach Boys Today/Summer Days (And Summer Nights) are presented in mono as they were originally recorded. No stereo versions of these albums exist.
- In late 1964 Brian Wilson quit touring to concentrate on writing and producing. The Beach Boys Today, a 1965 release, clearly reflected those efforts with a much more sophisticated and complete production.
- On Today, Brian put it all together…personal words, haunting melodies, stunningly complicated backing tracks and vocals of intricate beauty.
- *Summer Days (And Summer Nights)* continues to make significant leaps forward musically.
- Key tracks on *Summer Days (And Summer Nights)* include "Then I Kissed Her," "Help Me Rhonda" (single version), "California Girls," "Let Him Run Wild," "You're So Good To Me."
- Bonus tracks include "The Little Girl I Once Knew," "Dance, Dance, Dance" (early version), "I'm So Young," "Let Him Run Wild," "Graduation Day."

TRACKS: DO YOU WANNA DANCE; GOOD TO MY BABY; DON'T HURT MY LITTLE SISTER; WHEN I GROW UP (TO BE A MAN); HELP ME, RHONDA (LP VERSION); DANCE, DANCE, DANCE; PLEASE LET ME WONDER; I'M SO YOUNG; KISS ME BABY; SHE KNOWS ME TOO WELL; IN THE BACK OF MY MIND; BULL SESSION WITH "BIG DADDY"; THE GIRL FROM NEW YORK CITY; AMUSEMENT PARKS U.S.A.; THEN I KISSED HER; SALT LAKE CITY; GIRL DON'T TELL ME; HELP ME, RHONDA (SINGLE VERSION); CALIFORNIA GIRLS; LET HIM RUN WILD; YOU'RE SO GOOD TO ME; SUMMER MEANS NEW LOVE; I'M BUGGED AT MY OL' MAN; AND YOUR DREAMS COME TRUE; THE LITTLE GIRL I ONCE NEW (SINGLE)*; DANCE, DANCE, DANCE (ALTERNATE TAKE)*; I'M SO YOUNG (ALTERNATE TAKE)*; LET HIM RUN WILD (ALTERNATE TAKE)*; GRADUATION DAY (STUDIO VERSION)*

*BONUS TRACKS

Capitol

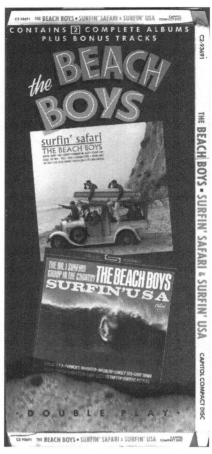

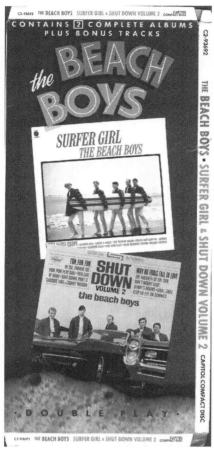

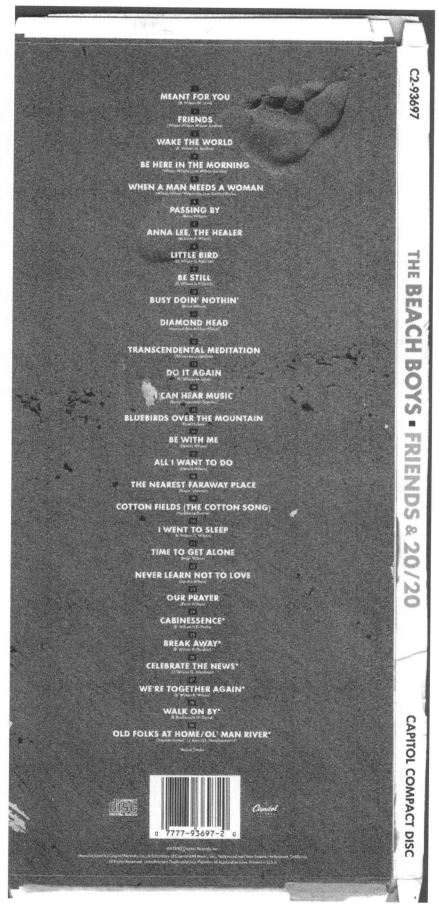

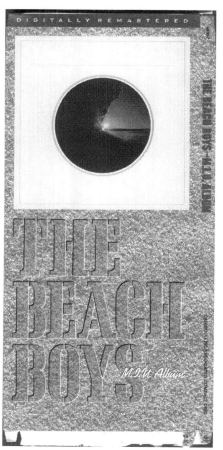

ROCK AND ROLL MUSIC

IT'S OK

HAD TO PHONE YA

CHAPEL OF LOVE

EVERYONE'S IN LOVE WITH YOU

TALK TO ME

THAT SAME SONG

T.M SONG

PALISADES PARK

SUSIE CINCINNATI

A CASUAL LOOK

BLUEBERRY HILL

BACK HOME

IN THE STILE OF THE NIGHT (I'LL REMEMBER)

JUST ONCE IN MY LIFE

The Beach Boys have the best sound in car stereo.

And the Beach Boys know sound.

Craig Powerplay's dual amplification produces over three times more power per channel than virtually any other car stereo. This componentry feature delivers clearer sound with less distortion at all volume levels. Not just more volume.

The Beach Boys' Powerplay car stereos are matched with Powerplay speakers, which are specifically designed to handle the extra power.

Get the best sound in car stereo and hear the Beach Boys' latest, "The Beach Boys Love You," on your own Craig Powerplay system. There are many models of Powerplay stereos and speakers to choose from.

For full details and specifications on the complete Powerplay line, write to Craig Corp., Dept. (A), P.O. Box 5864, 921 West Artesia Blvd., Compton, CA 90220. In Canada: Withers, Evans Ltd., 3133 Sumner Ave., Burnaby, B.C. V5G 3E3.

CRAIG
POWERPLAY
When you're serious about music.

To The Beach Boys:
Our Best Wishes for Continued Triumphs

Caribou Management Corporation

5 BIG ONES: (above)
1. Alan; 2. Brian; 3.
Michael; 4. Dennis; 5.
Carl.

1 5   B I G   O N E S

By JOEL SELVIN

It looks like this year will be the biggest in the 15-year history of The Beach Boys. The group starts its summer touring season over the Fourth of July weekend with stadium concerts in Oakland and Anaheim. Over the next three months The Beach Boys will perform before more than one million people.

A one-hour television special, to be produced by Emmy-winner Lorne Michaels of "Saturday Night," will be broadcast on Aug. 5 over NBC-TV. There are plans for a joint Carnegie Hall concert with the Joffrey Ballet, which has performed a suite of Beach Boys songs for several years.

BIG BROTHER IS BACK

Most important of all, the first new studio album by The Beach Boys in four years, "15 Big Ones," has been released by Reprise/Brother Records to coincide with the tour. "15 Big Ones" is a title that refers both to the number of cuts on the album and to the group's anniversary this year. It is also the first Beach Boys record in nine years to bear the legend: "Produced by Brian Wilson."

In a business where few acts make it back to the top after being there once and slipping, The Beach Boys achieved the impossible. In the decade since "Surfin' U.S.A.," a new generation grew up and found as much meaning in the surf and summer songs as did their older brothers and sisters 10 years ago.

Two summers ago, Capitol Records released a double-record set of 10-year-old Beach Boys recordings, "Endless Summer." The album shot straight to the top of the charts and turned gold. Last summer another Capitol double-record oldies set, "Spirit of America," earned another gold album. The sudden popularity of the old Beach Boys records was unprecedented in rock, and only a few years before, most of the Beach Boys LPs were cut out of the Capitol catalog.

For the last six years The Beach Boys worked extensively on the road, building the group's concert appeal to where a 12-city tour last summer with Chicago pulled more than $7 million at the boxoffice. Today The Beach Boys rank among the top concert attractions in rock.

But it has been four years since "Holland," the last Beach Boys studio album was released, and the time has never been more right for a new Beach Boys album. Many groups frankly influenced by The Beach Boys close harmony vocal style have come into their own, reflecting greatly on the orginators. Simple, positive songs, always the long suit of The Beach Boys, are experiencing renewed popularity. And, summer is here.

HIS WORK WAS DONE

In between the Cottage Thrift Shop on the corner and the parking lot across the street from the Santa Monica Greyhound station, Brother Studios hides behind an innocuous, anonymous exterior. Only two large philodendron plants flanking the front door outside give any hint of affluence.

Inside, however, gold Beach Boys albums line the walls. Out

SCHOOL DAYS 1949-50
York   SCHOOL DAYS 1949-50
York

track units in the compact control room. Equipment is all immediately accessible and ingeniously fitted into nooks and corners, including a miniaturized 1,500-hole patch bay.

After more than four months in the studio, sessions for the new album draw to a close early in May. One of the last sessions finds Carl Wilson mixing down the final version of "Everybody's In Love," a Mike Love song from the new album. Engineer Steve Moffitt is assisting, but it is Carl who actually operates the board. He gets the mix just about right in a little more than an hour and a half.

"Time to call in the brain trust," he says. The other Beach Boys are collected from various parts of the building. Mike Love, wearing a hat even inside the studio, hovers above the console, fiddling slightly with the knobs. Al Jardine settles back in the engineer's chair. As the tape begins to roll, Dennis Wilson pops his head inside the door and cocks his ear. He stays just long enough to make a comment and leave.

Love is concerned chiefly with the flute fills between verses (played by jazzman Charles Lloyd) and he takes over the flute track for the next mixdown. Jardine wants to hear more harp, but refuses to touch the board ("I just listen"), even when Carl offers.

The next time through does it. The mix is committed to the master tape, ready to go to the factory. The album would be finished in the next day or so.

"Where's Brian?" someone asks.

"Probably went back to where he came from," another answers. Older brother Brian Wilson has not been around the studio for the past couple days, but no one seems surprised. His work is done.

GENIUS OR LACK OF

"As a group we are democratic. Then we defer to Brian's judgment," Carl Wilson says, explaining the decision-making policy of The Beach Boys in the studio. An uncompromising artist, Brian Wilson has fashioned an album as certain to draw controversy as it is to sell a million. Since the group has been living, so to speak, on its own oldies of late, using other people's oldies for half the LP's material could be greeted either as a small stroke of genius or a total lack of originality. The customary smooth and polished Beach Boys vocal sound has been altered into something much more raw, vital and urgent. Precision gives way to immediacy.

For the album sessions The Beach Boys work on more than 30 different titles. Tape box lids lying around the studio turn up a number of the oldies titles not used on the album and they are tantilizing: "Sea Cruise," "Come Go With Me," "On Broadway," "Shake, Rattle And Roll," "Mony, Mony." A version of "Michael (Row The Boat Ashore)" is pulled from the album in its final stages.

The oldies on the album are Chuck Berry's "Rock And Roll Music" (the current single), the Dixie Cups' "Chapel Of Love,"

(Continued on page B-4)

GOOD VIBRATIONS: 1. Brian at work in 1966; 2. Dennis, age 1, and Brian, age 3½; 3. Mike and Al in 1975; 4. Dennis, age 5; 5. Brian, age 7½; 6. The Beach Boys in 1965.

1 5   B I G   O N E S

Sunny And The Sunglows' "Talk To Me," Freddie Cannon's "Palisades Park," the Six Teens' "A Casual Look," Fats Domino's "Blueberry Hill," the Five Satins' "In The Still Of The Night," and the Righteous Brothers' "Just Once In My Life."

Brian Wilson contributes five new original songs, which run from the summer-inspired fantasy "Back Home" and the summer credo "It's OK" to an interpretation of rock history, "That Same Song," a love song, "Had To Phone Ya," and the jingle-like "TM Song." Mike Love's "Everybody's In Love" and Al Jardine's "Suzie Cincinnati," a holdover from "Sunflower" days, complete the LP. The average song length is under 2½ minutes; the longest track just breaks 3½ minutes.

AND MIKE LOVE ON SAXOPHONE

The story of The Beach Boys has been told so many times in so many places, it begins to assume almost the status of a new American legend, and, indeed, their story is the stuff of modern myths. To date, The Beach Boys have sold some 75 million records and have outlasted any other group in pop music with the same members intact.

From the onset, Brian Wilson dominated the group. He formed the band in his senior year at Hawthorne High with his two brothers, Carl and Dennis, an older cousin, Mike Love, and a classmate, Al Jardine. The Wilsons were a musical family—the mother, Audrey, played organ at home, and the father, Murry, never gave up his aspirations as a songwriter—and the three boys grew up singing together. Audrey Wilson even played on the boys' first record, cut under the name Kenny and the Cadets by Hite Morgan, Murry Wilson's publisher.

It was Dennis Wilson, still the only surfer in the group, who convinced his land-locked brother Brian to write a song about the sport. Dennis, The Beach Boys' link to sea and surf, noticed the burgeoning popularity of surfing and described the whole scene in detail to Brian.

According to Carl Wilson, Al Jardine was interested in forming a folk group, a la the Kingston Trio, who were popular at the time. "The surfing group was a hot rumor around our house for months," the youngest Wilson brother said. He and Brian were the only members who already played instruments, so the other members were arbitrarily assigned axes: Dennis got drums; Al, who wanted to play bass, was convinced to take up rhythm guitar, as Brian took the bass and Carl the guitar. Mike Love was to play saxophone, but, somehow, that never worked out.

Called the Pendletones at the time, the group cut another record for Hite Morgan, Brian's composition "Surfin'," which became a Los Angeles-region hit, earned the group its name (given them allegedly by Russ Regan, president of 20th Century Records now, then a local promotion man for Candix Records), and landed the boys a contract with Capitol Records. The group's first Capitol single, "Surfin' Safari" and "409," was a nationwide hit and the surf music craze began.

Brian's talents blossomed. He wrote, arranged, produced, played and sang on all The Beach Boys records. His effortless falsetto immediately marked any of The Beach Boys ballads, as Mike Love, with his more nasal, middle-range voice, handled most of the rockers in the early days. Brian moved quickly from car and surf songs to subjects with broader scope, as his production and composition skills grew by leaps and bounds. The group's records never left the charts through 1963 and 1964, including seven consecutive top 10 singles.

Throughout his career, Brian wrote with a variety of lyricists, working, at first, with Gary Usher and Roger Christian on car songs like "409" or "Little Deuce Coupe." Mike Love has always been an important collaborator who shares many composer's credits with Brian ("Fun, Fun, Fun," "Warmth Of The Sun") and wrote three songs with him for "15 Big Ones." Brian also worked with Van Dyke Parks on the "Smile" album and Tony Asher on "Pet Sounds."

The Beach Boys played their first public performance New Year's Eve 1961 on a Ritchie Valens Memorial show at the Long Beach Auditorium. The group performed three songs, for which they were paid $300. A year later The Beach Boys had a top 15 record to their credit, their first album out, and teetered on the brink of the massive national success that was just weeks away.

At the time, the general thinking was that a hit pop group was good for two, at the most, three hit records and would last about a year. The Beach Boys made one LP for Capitol during their first year on the label. The next year the group made four albums. The intense release schedule, coupled with the gruelling schedule of concert appearances, took its toll on the relatively shy oldest Wilson brother.

(Continued on page B-6)

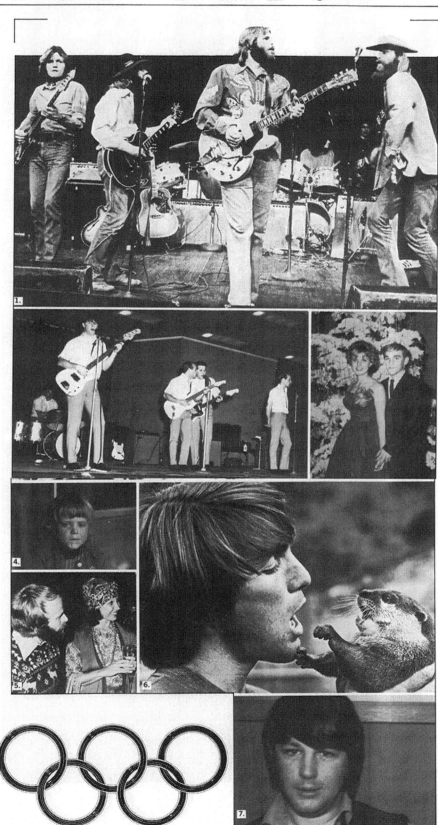

SURF'S UP: 1. Bruce Johnston, Al, Carl and Mike in concert in 1971; 2. Dennis (on drums), Brian, Al, Carl and Mike perform in 1963; 3. Dennis and a date at Hawthorne High's 1958 prom; 4. Al's oldest son; 5. Al and Linda Jardine in 1976; 6. Dennis in 1967; 7. Brian in 1966.

Happy Birthday, Sweet Fifteen!

Celebrate the best Beach Boys summer ever with 15 Big Ones. Featuring the smash hit "Rock and Roll Music," plus "It's OK" and 13 others. Produced by Brian Wilson. On Brother/Reprise records and tapes.

MS-2251

Brother records   REPRISE RECORDS   r

67

JULY 24, 1976, BILLBOARD

SPIRIT OF AMERICA: 1. Brian, Al and Brian's wife Marilyn in 1975; 2. Brian, Carl, a friend and Dennis in Hawthorne in 1950; 3. Brian in 1959; 4. Brian at 2 weeks in the arms of father Murry Wilson, 1942; 5. Mike (white hat) and (descending) Alan, Bruce Johnston, Dennis, and Carl.

1 5   B I G   O N E S

PET SOUNDS, BEFORE ITS TIME

Brian suffered a nervous breakdown at age 21 on an airplane trip to Houston two days before Christmas 1964. The strain of doing everything proved too much. Shortly after, he retired from touring with The Beach Boys to concentrate on making the group's records. He was replaced on the road at first by Glen Campbell and, later, by Bruce Johnston, who made surfing records (with producer Terry Melcher) as Bruce & Terry. Johnston remained with The Beach Boys six years.

After he quit touring, Brian began to experiment with orchestration, ultimately leading to his 1966 masterpiece, "Pet Sounds," an album far ahead of its time and misunderstood in its day. No pop producer before, not even Phil Spector, had marshalled such lush, ambitious arrangements, and the fact that the album didn't outsell the group's earlier efforts was a blow from which Brian never recovered.

He immersed himself for the next year recording an album with Van Dyke Parks that was to be an even more ambitious project. He was locked in some unspoken competition with the Beatles, who had yet to release "Sergeant Pepper," and whispered rumors of the grand scale of the "Smile" album added to its pre-release reputation.

In October 1966, with no sign of "Smile" in sight, The Beach Boys released "Good Vibrations," which became the group's first million-selling single, Brian's definitive piece, and remains to this day The Beach Boys' biggest selling single. Without explanation, "Smile" was scrapped. In its place came "Smiley Smile," an album recorded in about two weeks, with "Good Vibrations" on it. "Smiley Smile' was a bunt," Carl Wilson says, "instead of a grand slam." For the first time the credit on the LP read: "Produced by The Beach Boys."

Brian retreated to his Bel-Air mansion, where he set up a studio in his living room and recorded the next Beach Boys album, "Wild Honey." "When we did 'Wild Honey,' " Carl says, "Brian asked me to get more involved in the recording end. He wanted a break. He was tired. He had been doing it all too long."

RESISTANCE WORE THIN

As Brian receded from total control of the group, other members stepped forward. On the next album, "Friends," Al Jardine and Dennis Wilson entered the picture as important songwriting factors in the group, as Carl took a more active role in producing.

The emergence of FM "underground" radio, along with San Francisco bands like the Grateful Dead and British groups like Cream, pushed The Beach Boys out of the limelight. Always essentially a "singles" band, The Beach Boys had to withstand a period where that ran against the hip esthetic.

Nevertheless, the cultural ferment of the period did not leave the group untouched. Carl Wilson was indicted for his refusal to be inducted by the draft, and courts considered the validity of his conscientious objector's status for years before clearing him.

In 1967 the group began their continuing involvement with transcendental meditation after meeting the Mahareshi Mahesh Yogi in Paris. The Beach Boys performed before nearly 500,000 protestors at the 1971 May Day demonstrations in Washington. Later that year the group cancelled part of a tour to play a benefit concert for the Berrigan brothers defense fund.

Philosophy entered the business scene too, as The Beach Boys established their own record company, Brother Records, a "non-business concept" that released "Smiley Smile" through Capitol, before disappearing, only to be pulled out of mothballs once the group changed labels.

In 1970, after seven years with Capitol, The Beach Boys signed with Warner Bros. and reactivated the Brother label. The release of an outstanding LP, "Sunflower," that year, and subsequent live appearances at Hollywood's Whiskey a Go Go (where Brian joined the group onstage briefly for the first time since Houston) and the Big Sur Folk Festival helped establish the group's credibility with the counter-culture. In April 1971 when the Beach Boys joined the Grateful Dead onstage at Fillmore East for a jam session, such acceptance became a certainty.

Resistance began to wear thin by the time the "Surf's Up" LP was released in late 1971. The album included the famed title track, which Brian performed five years before on a network television special hosted by Leonard Bernstein and originally intended to be part of the "Smile" album, which he was recording when the tv special was filmed.

Politics also reared its head on "Surf's Up." For the first time, The Beach Boys took note of such social concerns as pollution, health and nutrition, and student demonstrations, in songs such as "Don't Go Near The Water" or "Student Demonstration Time."

The group spent virtually all of 1972, and a small personal fortune recording the last Beach Boys studio album, "Holland," in the Netherlands. Blondie Chaplin and Ricky Fataar, former members of South African rock band Flame that Carl Wilson produced for Brother Records (the only non-Beach Boys album ever released by Brother), went along as members of the band.

After recording facilities in the European country were found inadequate to the group's needs, The Beach Boys shipped an entire 24-track studio, piece-by-piece, from the West Coast. Every Los Angeles-Amsterdam flight for three months carried something to The Beach Boys, sometimes just a tiny part. When it was all assembled and turned on for the first time, smoke poured out of the board.

(Continued on page B-8)

68

Congratulations to the legends of American Music

Steve Wolf · Jim Rissmiller · Larry Vallon

ENDLESS SUMMER: 1. Brian relaxes in 1976; 2. Dennis in '75; 3. Carl in '75; 4. Carl age 8;

5. Dennis, age 10; 6. Brian, age 7; 7. Dennis in 1963.

1 5   B I G   O N E S

Over the next three years the group built its following through literally hundreds of concerts. A double record set of old hits recorded live earned a gold album six months before the first Capitol re-release set was issued. That was the last regular release album from The Beach Boys until now. Last summer Reprise/Brother put out "Good Vibrations," a reissue album of later Beach Boys cuts, in addition to the two Capitol sets. "We knew about the reissues," Mike Love explains, "and we had the sense that we should stay out of their way."

Constant touring boosted The Beach Boys to the top ranks of contemporary rock concert attractions, capped by the joint tour last summer with Chicago and the Wembley Stadium concert with Elton John, at which most British critics agreed The Beach Boys surpassed the titular headline act. A new generation of teenagers discovered The Beach Boys and, with Brian Wilson back at the helm of the group's recordings, The Beach Boys have returned to full strength, ready to do it again.

KEEPIN' IT IN THE FAMILY

One key to the longevity of The Beach Boys is the family connection. Mike Love's mother was Murry Wilson's sister, making him a cousin to the Wilson brothers. His brother Steve Love manages The Beach Boys currently and his other brother Stan Love, a 6 foot 9 inch former NBA forward, also works for the group. His sister Maureen played harp on the new album, her first appearance on a Beach Boys record since "Catch A Wave." Carl Wilson's brother-in-law Billy Hinsche, once a member of Dino, Desi & Billy, also worked on the new album and plays in the band on tour.

All three Wilson brothers are married (Dennis married for the third time last month) and have children. They all still live in the Los Angeles area. Denny and Carl on the beach. Mike Love resides in Santa Barbara overlooking the ocean and Al Jardine lives on a ranch near Big Sur where he has installed a recording studio.

All The Beach Boys and many of their associates practice transcendental meditation in some form; Mike Love and Al Jardine are TM teachers. Even Beach Boy engineer Steve Moffitt meditates. Brother Studios comes equipped with a meditation room. Brian contributed an original to the new album, "TM Song," singing the praises of the mental discipline advocated by the Maharishi Mahesh Yogi. "I wrote the song for the Maharishi," Brian told a San Francisco press conference held to celebrate the new album, "and I hope he hears it. His method for cultivating the mind is so advanced, it merited at least a couple songs." Indeed, "TM Song" coupled with "Transcendental Meditation" from the "Friends" LP, makes for the second Beach Boys song to extol the virtues of TM.

DEAN ONCE SANG LEAD

A lot of studio musicians who played on "15 Big Ones" were veterans of previous Beach Boys records. Daryl Dragon and Toni Tennille, former Beach Boys band members known professionally now as the Captain & Tennille, sang backgrounds on Mike Love's "Everybody's In Love" on the new album. Even the album cover and new logo were designed by an old friend, Dean Torrence, who runs Kittyhawk Graphics now, but was once one-half of the surf and car singing duo Jan & Dean. Brian Wilson co-wrote many Jan & Dean hits in the heyday of the surf/car craze ("Drag City," "New Girl In School," "Dead Man's Curve") and Torrence once sang lead on a Beach Boys record ("Barbara Ann").

I FEEL MORE SECURE AT HOME

A month ago The Beach Boys staged an extravagant press affair in San Francisco to celebrate the new album. All the group members attended—including reclusive Brian, participating in his first Beach Boys press function anyone could remember.

About 60 members of the press, radio and television were assembled and waiting in the Presidential Suite of the Sheraton Inn-Fisherman's Wharf when Brian Wilson strode in and made a beeline for the small room where the television lights and photographers waited.

Wringing his hands and nervously tapping his toes, Brian sat straight as a pole, obviously uncomfortable, but smiling bravely. Al Jardine missed his flight, but the interview began anyway.

"I read in the background material," the tv interviewer starts, "that you don't care much for touring, going out on the road or doing interviews like this . . ."

"No. I feel more secure at home," Brian jumps in, "where I can do sketchworks for albums, sketching out songs, calling up Paul McCartney, being on an ego trip. Something where there's some kind of ego involved keeps me going." People listen intently, taking him seriously, and Brian warms to his task.

"Elton John was over at my house . . . Andy Williams, I get this feeling, I think, hey, I like it here." The other Beach Boys start chuckling.

"I like to get that social thing moving," Brian continues, as the laughter accelerates. "In fact," he declares, "I think it's healthy to meet stars. . . . Hey! What's so funny?"

After the television crew finishes, the press breaks into four separate rooms for individual interviews with one of four Beach Boys, as Brian roams room-to-room at his whim. He joins Mike Love and a dozen or so reporters in one room and holds court briefly with the same combination of excitement, bluster and nervousness he exhibited before the tv cameras. He fields a question about how he selects lead singers for specific songs among the Beach Boys.

(Continued on page B-76)

Happy
15
Big Ones!

Rogers & Cowan, Inc.

The Beach Boys

ON TOUR

7/2 Oakland Stadium, Oakland, California	8/29 Stadium, Hartford, Connecticut
7/3 Anaheim Stadium, Anaheim, California	8/30-31 Capitol Center, Washington, D.C.
7/12-14 Pine Knob Theater, Detroit, Michigan	9/1 Nassau Coliseum, Hempstead, L.I., New York
7/15-17 Chicago Stadium, Chicago, Illinois	9/2 Erie Stadium, Erie, Pennsylvania
7/18 Mile High Stadium, Denver, Colorado	9/3-4 Canadian National Exhibition, Toronto, Canada
7/21 Edmonton Coliseum, Edmonton, Alberta, Canada	9/5 Civic Center, Ontario, Canada
7/23 Arrowhead Stadium, Kansas City, Missouri	9/6 Forum, Montreal, Quebec, Canada
7/24 Wisconsin State Fair, Milwaukee, Wisconsin	9/14 *To be announced*
7/25 Iowa State Fair Park Raceway, Des Moines, Iowa	9/16 Brigham Young University, Provo, Utah
8/6 Parade Stadium, Minneapolis, Minnesota	9/18 Dome Stadium, Seattle, Washington
8/8 Kiel Auditorium, St. Louis, Missouri	9/19-20 Canadian National Exhibition, Vancouver, Canada
8/11-12 Spectrum, Philadelphia, Pennsylvania	9/21 Coliseum, Portland, Oregon
8/13 Coliseum, Hampton Roads, Virginia	9/24 Coliseum, San Diego, California
8/14 Three Rivers Stadium, Pittsburgh, Pennsylvania	9/25 Hughes Stadium, Sacramento, California
8/15 Columbus, Ohio	9/26 Stadium, Santa Barbara, California
8/26 Music Center, Saratoga Springs, New York	10/1 Mid-South Coliseum, Memphis, Tennessee
8/27 Rich Stadium, *(tentative)*, Buffalo, New York	10/2 Barton Coliseum, Little Rock, Arkansas
8/28 Roosevelt Stadium, Jersey City, New Jersey	10/3 Tulsa State Fair, Tulsa, Oklahoma

ICM
INTERNATIONAL CREATIVE MANAGEMENT

D I S C O G R A P H Y

SINGLES

Dates Released	Position	Weeks	Title	Label
2/17/62	75	6	SURFIN	Candix 331
8/11/62	14	17	SURFIN' SAFARI	Capitol 4777
10/13/62	76	1	409	Capitol 4777
12/1/62	49	8	TEN LITTLE INDIANS	Capitol 4880
3/23/63	3	17	°SURFIN' U.S.A.	Capitol 4932
4/27/63	23	13	SHUT DOWN	Capitol 4932
8/3/63	7	14	°SURFER GIRL	Capitol 5009
8/17/63	15	11	LITTLE DEUCE COUPE	Capitol 5009
11/2/63	6	12	°BE TRUE TO YOUR SCHOOL	Capitol 5069
11/2/63	23	11	IN MY ROOM	Capitol 5069
2/15/64	5	11	°FUN, FUN, FUN	Capitol 5118
5/23/64	1	15	°°I GET AROUND	Capitol 5174
5/30/64	24	10	DON'T WORRY BABY	Capitol 5174
9/5/64	9	10	°WHEN I GROW UP (TO BE A MAN)	Capitol 5245
10/17/64	44	6	WENDY	Capitol E.P. 5267
10/17/64	65	5	LITTLE HONDA	Capitol E.P. 5267
11/7/64	8	11	°DANCE, DANCE, DANCE	Capitol 5306
2/27/65	12	8	DO YOU WANNA DANCE?	Capitol 5372
3/6/65	52	5	PLEASE LET ME WONDER	Capitol 5372
4/17/65	1	14	°°HELP ME, RHONDA	Capitol 5395
7/24/65	3	11	°CALIFORNIA GIRLS	Capitol 5464
11/27/65	20	8	THE LITTLE GIRL I ONCE KNEW	Capitol 5540
1/1/66	2	11	°BARBARA ANN	Capitol 5561
4/2/66	3	11	°SLOOP JOHN B	Capitol 5602
7/30/66	8	11	°WOULDN'T IT BE NICE	Capitol 5706
8/13/66	39	8	GOD ONLY KNOWS	Capitol 5706
10/22/66	1	14	°°GOOD VIBRATIONS	Capitol 5676
8/5/67	12	7	HEROES AND VILLAINS	Brother 1001
11/4/67	31	6	WILD HONEY	Capitol 2028
12/23/67	19	9	DARLIN'	Capitol 2068
4/20/68	47	7	FRIENDS	Capitol 2160
7/27/68	20	10	DO IT AGAIN	Capitol 2239
12/14/68	61	6	BLUEBIRDS OVER THE MOUNTAIN	Capitol 2360
3/8/69	24	10	I CAN HEAR MUSIC	Capitol 2432
7/5/69	63	6	BREAK AWAY	Capitol 2530
3/7/70	64	5	ADD SOME MUSIC TO YOUR DAY	Reprise 0894
10/30/71	89	5	LONG PROMISED ROAD	Brother/Reprise 1047
2/24/73	79	7	SAIL ON SAILOR	Brother 1138
5/12/73	84	4	CALIFORNIA SAGA (ON MY WAY TO SUNNY CALIFORN-I-A)	Brother 1156
8/17/74	36	8	SURFIN' U.S.A.	Capitol 3924
4/12/75	49	10	SAIL ON SAILOR	Reprise/Brother 1325
6/5/76	. . .	. . .	°ROCK'N'ROLL MUSIC	Warner/Reprise/Brother 1354

ALBUMS

Dates Released	Position	Weeks	Title	Label
11/24/62	32	37	SURFIN' SAFARI	Capitol 1808
5/4/63	2	78	°SURFIN' U.S.A.	Capitol 1890
10/12/63	7	56	°SURFER GIRL	Capitol 1981
11/9/63	4	46	°LITTLE DEUCE COUPE	Capitol 1998
4/11/64	13	38	SHUT DOWN—VOL. 2	Capitol 2027
8/1/64	4	49	°ALL SUMMER LONG	Capitol 2110
11/7/64	1	62	°°THE BEACH BOYS' CONCERT	Capitol 2198
3/27/65	4	50	°THE BEACH BOYS TODAY	Capitol 2269
7/24/65	2	33	°SUMMER DAYS (AND SUMMER NIGHTS)	Capitol 2354
11/27/65	6	24	°THE BEACH BOYS' PARTY	Capitol 2398
5/28/66	10	39	°PET SOUNDS	Capitol 2458
7/23/66	8	78	°BEST OF THE BEACH BOYS—VOL. 1	Capitol 2545
8/12/67	50	22	BEST OF THE BEACH BOYS—VOL. 2	Capitol 2706
9/30/67	41	21	SMILEY SMILE	Brother 9001
12/30/67	24	15	WILD HONEY	Capitol 2859
7/6/68	126	10	FRIENDS	Capitol 2895
9/7/68	153	6	BEST OF THE BEACH BOYS—VOL. 3	Capitol 2945
3/1/69	68	11	20/20	Capitol 133
8/16/69	136	6	CLOSE UP	Capitol 253
9/26/70	151	4	SUNFLOWER	Reprise 6382
9/11/71	29	17	SURF'S UP	Reprise 6453
6/3/72	50	20	PET SOUNDS/CARL & THE PASSIONS "SO TOUGH"	Reprise 2083
1/27/73	36	25	HOLLAND	Reprise 2118
12/8/73	25	19	THE BEACH BOYS IN CONCERT	Reprise 6484
7/20/74	1	74	°°ENDLESS SUMMER ■	Capitol 11307
8/3/74	50	11	WILD HONEY & 20/20	Reprise 2166
9/11/74	125	6	FRIENDS & SMILEY SMILE	Reprise 2167
5/3/75	8	30	SPIRIT OF AMERICA	Capitol 11384
5/31/75	158	5	HOLLAND	Reprise/Brother 2118
7/19/75	25	16	GOOD VIBRATIONS—BEST OF THE BEACH BOYS	Reprise/Brother 2223
7/10/76	. . .	. . .	15 BIG ONES	Warner Bros. 2251

Reprinted by permission of Joel Whitburn's Record Research
°° = No. 1
° = Top 10
■ = Active on charts
. . . = See current charts

The Beach Boys

would like to thank

Westwood Music-

Fred Walecki,

the expertise
of John Carruthers

and extra special thanks
to Mike Huber
for his assistance.

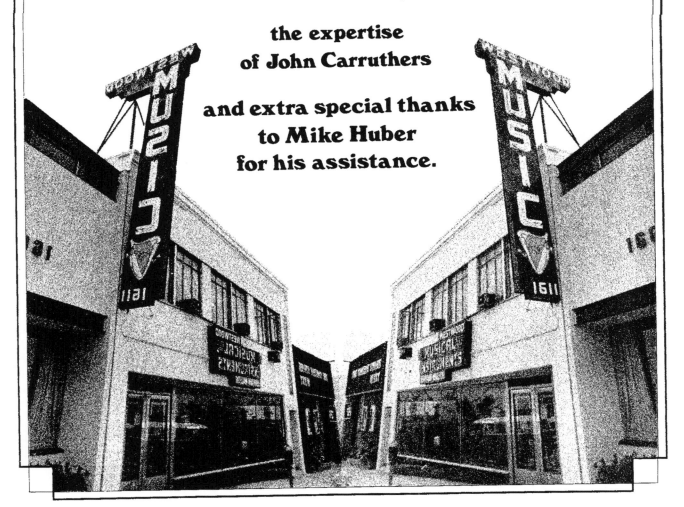

In any land
In any language
THE BEACH BOYS are success.

WEA International proudly salutes the career that grows more illustrious every year.

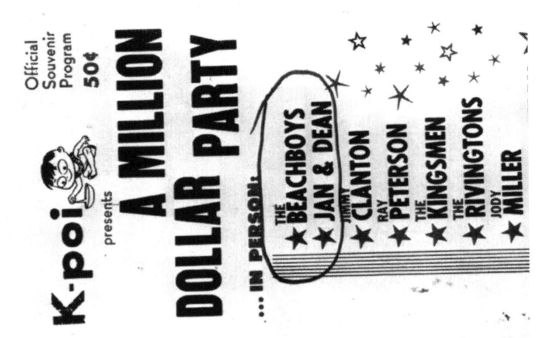

15 BIG ONES

"I know their voices and I know which one is right for what song," he says. "There's no politics in The Beach Boys. There's no grappling for leads like there is in other major groups. Some of the well known groups really like to grapple for leads. And Three Dog Night, who, as you know, broke up. Now Danny Hutton is solo and the other two are Two Dog Night.... What's so funny? If I brought a comedian in here you'd probably cry."

Later in the evening The Beach Boys host about 100 friends and associates to a performance by the Joffrey Ballet at the War Memorial Opera House. Most of the band members have never seen the ballet dance to their music before. After the performance the party repairs for a late night supper at San Francisco's swank French restaurant Ernie's, where the party continues past midnight.

SUMMER MEANS NEW LOVE

Carl Wilson understands Brian making people laugh easily from when they were children. "We all slept in the same room," he says, "and after we went to bed, Brian would sit there trying to make us laugh. First, my mother would come in and warn us. If our father came in, then it was curtains. So we'd be trying not to laugh, covering our mouths, hiding under the sheets, and Brian would keep cracking us up."

Humor has always been an important part of Brian Wilson's music—whether it is the outright cut-up cuts like "'Cassius' Love vs 'Sony' Wilson" and "Bull Session With The 'Big Daddy'" from early albums, or the gentle whimsy of "I'd Love Just Once To See You" from "Wild Honey." Brian's humor extends to his arrangements or even instrumental sounds on the rhythm tracks, like the groaning organ in "Chapel Of Love" on the new album.

Along with humor, another prominent thread through Brian's music is his positive point of view. Essentially uncritical, Brian's compositions focus on happy endings, joyful and innocent romance, universal activities that bring people together. With his child-like sensibilties, he breathes life into ostensibly stereotyped and even trite emotional situations, not unlike painter Norman Rockwell. He has also confronted more complex emotional situations, as on "Pet Sounds," with deep feeling and sensitivity.

Brian's musical imagination—along with Mike Love's lyr-
(Continued on page B-24)

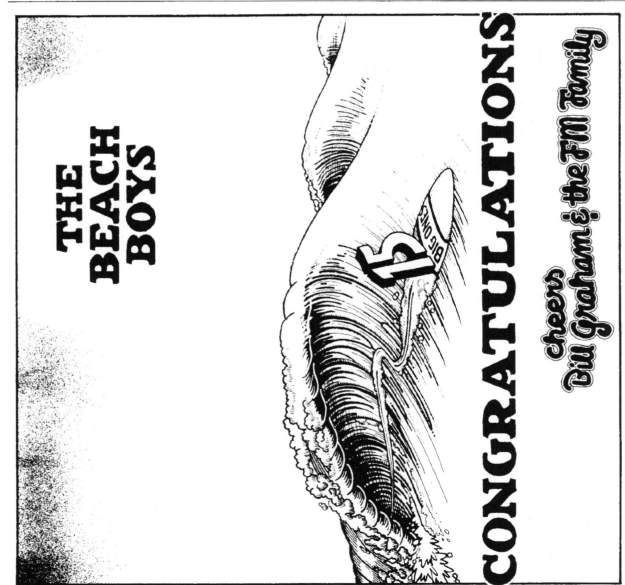

THE BEACH BOYS

CONGRATULATIONS

cheers
Bill Graham & the FM Family

Just Released In The U.K.!

THE BEACH BOYS
20 GOLDEN GREATS

Congratulations,
The Beach Boys,
on 15 years
of wonderful music!

Capitol
A Division of EMI Records, Limited

Friday Evening, September 24, 1971 at 7:30 and 11:00

CARNEGIE HALL/80th Anniversary Season

RON DELSENER

presents

THE BEACH BOYS

CARL WILSON   AL JARDINE   BRUCE JOHNSTON   MIKE LOVE   DENNIS WILSON

Mike Kowalski
Eddie Carter
Bobby Torres
Ricky Fataar
Daryl Dragon

Joel Peskin
Roger Newman
Sal Marquez
Glenn Ferris
Mike Price

You're my Pet Sounds

Gus Dudgeon

THANKS FOR 8 BIG ONES!

*Bruce
Johnston*

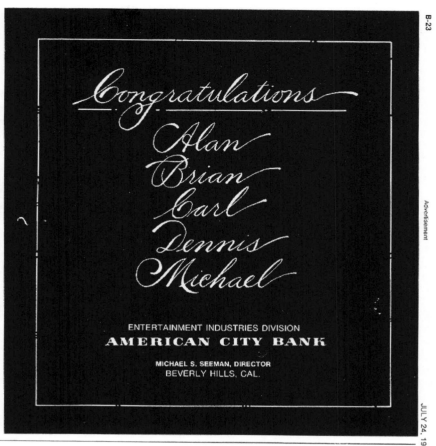

15 BIG ONES

ics—encapsulated the sun and surf world of California in the early '60s in a handful of songs—like "Catch A Wave," "Fun, Fun, Fun," "Little Deuce Coupe," "I Get Around," "California Girls"—with as much accuracy and insight as any novelist could. Songs such as "In My Room" or "When I Grow Up" expressed an incredible empathy with the alienation and introspection that is a natural part of adolescence.

Stylistically, Brian drew from the vocal harmonies of the Four Freshmen, in addition to rhythm & blues vocal groups, to create The Beach Boys vocal sound. In his production style he was greatly influenced by Phil Spector and the girl group records of the '60s Spector made with the Crystals and the Ronettes on his Philles Records label. Brian even used some of the same studio musicians as Spector on his records. He drew on Chuck Berry for the Beach Boys 1963 hit, "Surfin' U.S.A." and the rock'n'roll guitar introduction to "Fun, Fun, Fun."

Brian shattered a lot of precedents in the recording industry. Not only was he the first important rock musician to produce his own records for a major label, but he was the first pop artist to commit himself completely to the quality of his work.

Producer Nick Venet, who signed the group to Capitol and was the titular producer of the group's first records, told "Rolling Stone": "Brian was one of the first acts on a major label to bust out of the major label syndrome of coming in their studios at their appointed hours and using their facilities—good, bad or indifferent—at their union scales and their hours. . . . He was also the first guy to do it until it was right. He damned everyone till it was right and then he gave them the record. He took his chances. A lot of us would get chicken after four hours and say 'We'd better get off the tune.' Brian would hang in there for nine hours, no matter what the cost. I used to think he was crazy, but he was right."

The fifth Beach Boys album, "Shut Down, Volume Two," which was released in February 1964, just as "I Want To Hold Your Hand" shot into the top 10 and the Beatles arrived in the U.S. for the first time, is often cited as the first rock concept album. "Shut Down, Volume One" was a stock Capitol various artists package that threw together a selection of car songs. The Beach Boys' "Volume Two" combined automotive rockers like "Fun, Fun, Fun" ("She got her daddy's car . . . ."), "This Car Of Mine," and "In The Parking Lot" with two re-

(Continued on page B-26)

CREDITS

Editor, Earl Paige. Story by Joel Selvin, music critic, San Francisco Chronicle. Creative direction, Rogers & Cowan. Art, Dean Torrence. Kittyhawk Production. John Halloran.

15 BIG ONES

markably eloquent (but simple) ballads. "Don't Worry Baby" and "Warmth Of The Sun," plus typical surf band instrumentals ("Shut Down—Part Two," "Denny's Drums").

Donald Lyons in the March 1967 issue of "Hullabaloo Magazine" wrote: "What are cars and surfboards? They are primary colors of American motion. Cars are an active exploitation of natural energy through the machine, and surfboards a passive enjoyment of natural energy through bodily skill—two brilliantly characteristic modes of American response to life. And the Beach Boys, in their earlier music, seize the joy, the gladness, the rhythms of these machines as no one else has."

But, of course, Brian took it much further. He just started with car and surf songs. Before long, he created a whole myth world on his records out of southern California—where summer means new love. "California Girls" may have been his ultimate West Coast fantasy.

On "15 Big Ones," more than a decade later, Brian is still dealing with mythology—his own and that of rock'n'roll. "A lot of people have grown up since these songs were hits." Brian said about the oldies on the album, "and never heard them before. So these are just like new songs to them." The renditions of songs like "Blueberry Hill" or "In The Still Of The Night" clearly indicate Brian's awareness of the classic proportions of both the material and his group. His originals, like "Back Home," "It's OK," or "That Same Song," help supply the necessary perspective.

Without being nostalgic, the album gently suggests rock's future may lie in its past. "15 Big Ones" seems intent on preserving the innocent, timeless quality of great rock music. No one on the scene today is better equipped to point the way in that direction than The Beach Boys.

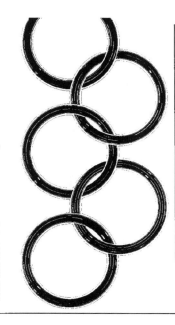

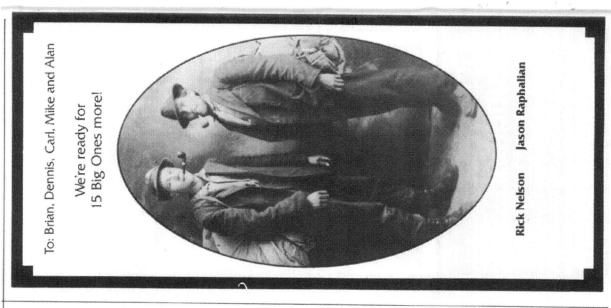

The Beach Boys
The Beach Boys
The Beach Boys
The Beach Boys
The Beach Boys
The Beach Boys
The Beach Boys
The Beach Boys
The Beach Boys
The Beach Boys
The Beach Boys
The Beach Boys
The Beach Boys
The Beach Boys
The Beach Boys
The Beach Boys
The Beach Boys
The Beach Boys
The Beach Boys
The Beach Boys

Roger Christian was there when it all started happening for THE BEACH BOYS. He wrote over 50 of the songs they and Jan & Dean recorded. No one else can ever recapture those fabulous beach years as he has in this four-hour musical spectacular.

THE BEACH BOYS is dynamite summertime listening! It's now available for markets of all sizes, and for stereo or non-stereo stations. The program was written, produced and hosted by Roger Christian and Jim Pewter, a Billboard Program Director of the Year award winner. Roger Christian received the RIAA Gold Album Award for producing Capitol Records' "The Beatles Story." He brings the same talent to this unique story of THE BEACH BOYS, which also recalls such other surfing greats as The Surfaris, Jan & Dean and Dick Dale.

With a total of 48 commercial availabilities, this is one special your Sales Department won't want to miss! If you'd like some idea of the excitement THE BEACH BOYS can generate for you, please mail the coupon below to receive our free demonstration record...or call Darwin Lamm collect at (213) 276-5022.

Creative Radio Shows
912 i Sunset Blvd.
Los Angeles, Calif. 90069
(213) 276-5022

TO: CREATIVE RADIO SHOWS
912 i Sunset Blvd., Los Angeles, Calif. 90069
I'd like to hear a sample of your musical spectacular, THE BEACH BOYS.
Please send me your free demonstration record.

NAME:

TITLE: PHONE:

ADDRESS:

CITY: STATE: STATION:

                                            ZIP:

BRIAN WILSON of the BEACH BOYS

"THE BEACH BOYS: AN AMERICAN BAND" is a musical profile of The Beach Boys' 24-year career capturing the excitement of their music, the story of their private lives and the group's impact on American Culture. Pictured: (Left to Right: Al Jardine, Bruce Johnston, Brian Wilson, Mike Love, and Carl Wilson.

"THE BEACH BOYS: AN AMERICAN BAND" is a musical profile of The Beach Boys' 24-year career capturing the excitement of their music, the story of their private lives and the group's impact on American Culture.

"THE BEACH BOYS: AN AMERICAN BAND" is a musical profile of The Beach Boys' 24-year career capturing the excitement of their music, the story of their private lives and the group's impact on American Culture. Pictured: (Left to Right) Al Jardine, Bruce Johnston, Dennis Wilson, Carl Wilson, and Mike Love.

"THE BEACH BOYS: AN AMERICAN BAND" is a musical profile of The Beach Boys' 24-year career capturing the excitement of their music, the story of their private lives and the group's impact on American Culture. Pictured: Brian Wilson.

"THE BEACH BOYS: AN AMERICAN BAND" is a musical profile of The Beach Boys' 24-year career capturing the excitement of their music, the story of their private lives and the group's impact on American Culture.

102

WRITTEN AND DIRECTED BY MALCOLM LEO

PRODUCED BY
MALCOLM LEO AND BONNIE PETERSON

EXECUTIVE PRODUCERS
JON PEISINGER AND MICHAEL WIESE

EDITED BY DAVID FAIRFIELD

CO-EDITOR MARK COLE

ASSOCIATE PRODUCERS
RON FURMANEK   RANDY GLADSTEIN

TECHNICAL ADVISORS
TOM HULETT   JERRY SCHILLING

PRODUCTION EXECUTIVE ROUBEN RAPELIAN

CLEARANCE ADMINISTRATOR VICKI GRIMSLAND

ASSISTANT EDITOR KARL JACOBSEN

PRODUCTION ASSISTANT EDICK HOSSEPIAN

FILM & VIDEOTAPE RESEARCH
PAUL SURRATT   JOHN DELGATTO

AUDIO RESEARCH RON FURMANEK

RESEARCH DENNIS DIKEN

DIRECTOR OF PHOTOGRAPHY JOHN TOLL

ADDITIONAL PHOTOGRAPHY FRITZ ROLAND

LOCATION SOUND BRUCE BISENZ

VIDEOTAPE EDITORS
LARRY HARRIS   PAM MARSHALL
FRANK MAZZARO   MARK WEST
ANDY ZALL

AUDIO DOUG NELSON

STUDIO SOUND COORDINATOR PEGGY SANDVIG

MAIN TITLE GRAPHICS CHARLES MCDONALD

PRODUCTION COORDINATOR KATHIE VAN BRUNT

PRODUCTION SECRETARIES
DESERT COWART   LUCINDA DRONBERGER

ASSISTANTS TO THE EXECUTIVE PRODUCERS
CAROL KAPITAN   KATHERINE GOULD

A MALCOLM LEO FILM

THE PRODUCERS GRATEFULLY ACKNOWLEDGE:

JOHN G. BRANCA	BILLY HINSCHE	GINA MARTIN	GARY STIFFELMAN	ANNIE WILSON
KIP BROWN	CRAIG JACOBSON	RICCI MARTIN	MISTY THOMAS	BARBARA WILSON
MICHAEL CHAVEZ	HAL JEPSEN	RON NICKELL	GEORGE VAN NOY	CAROLE WILSON
BRAD ELLIOTT	HARRIET JOHNSTON	DAVID OPPENHEIM	JOHN VINCENT	MARILYN WILSON
JIM FITZPATRICK	KAREN LAMM	VAN DYKE PARKS	SUSAN F. WALKER	DON WINFREY
JAMES W. GUERCIO	EUGENE LANDY	JASON RAPHALIAN	SANDY WERNICK	WALTER WINNICK
TOM HANSEN	IRIS MARCH	ED ROACH	AUDREE WILSON	BROADWAY VIDEO

RESEARCH VIDEO

CARIBOU RANCH, COLORAD

POST PRODUCTION FACILITIES COMPLETE POST, INC.

A HIGH RIDGE PRODUCTION
IN ASSOCIATION WITH
MALCOLM LEO PRODUCTIONS

RUNNING TIME: 103 MINUTE

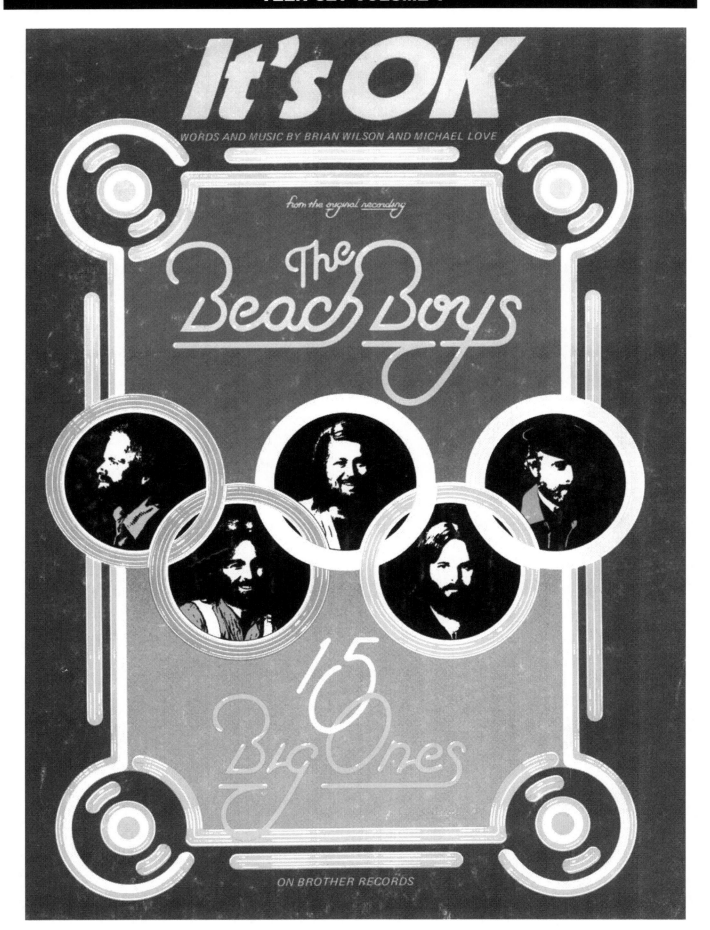

The Philadelphia Phonograph

RECORD MAGAZINE
Free From WMMR

Vol. 6 No. 8   JUNE, 1976

AMERICA CELEBRATES THE BEACH BOYS

The Most Influential Band The U.S. Has Ever Produced

By KEN BARNES
PRM Staff Writer

The Beach Boys have come of age. 1976 is their 15th anniversary, and they and their fans are celebrating it with a six-month tour, criss-crossing the nation playing to sold-out crowds in 50-90,000 capacity stadium sites. Their first new studio album in over three years, "15 Big Ones," will be out in July, and from all indications (including an advance audition-see inside story), it will be a colossal hit. With "15 Big Ones" and its first single hit "Rock And Roll Music," the Beach Boys are serving notice that they're ready to have fun again, in the studio as well as on stage, and the whole country will be ready and willing to follow their lead. The summer days (and summer nights) of 1976 will be filled with Beach Boys action, in concert, on record, in magazines, on TV and on the radio. By the end of this Bicentennial (and 15th anniversary) year, the Beach Boys should find themselves, once again, the reigning American band. It's their year for Number One.

(See story page 24)

Feature Index

Derringer-Page 19
Steve Miller-Page 33
Dr. Feelgood-Page 18
Miles Davis-Page 36
Isley Bros.-Page 37

New Beatles LP For States

See Story Page 13.

BUST YOUR BUNS

107

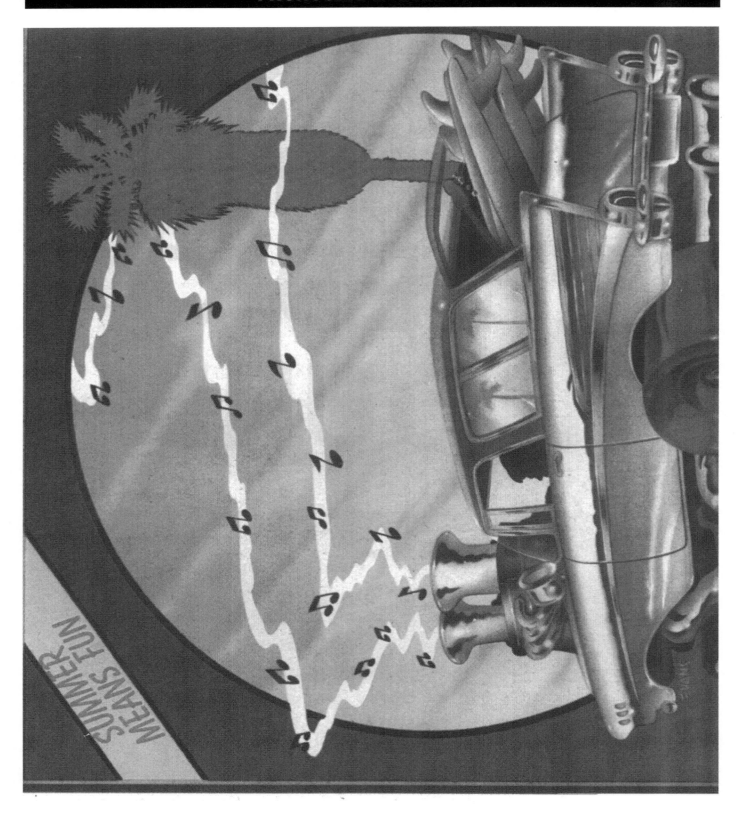

THE BEACH BOYS AND THAT ★ CALIFORNIA ★ SOUND

ERIC CARMEN:

"They are certainly the most important and influential band America has ever produced. Melodically brilliant songwriting, complex arrangements and complete control of the recording studio combine to make the music interesting, inspiring, and yet always accessible. Their vocal harmonies are unsurpassed....I think Brian was a french horn, Carl was a flute, Al Jardine a trumpet, Dennis a trombone, and Mike Love a baritone-sax before their present incarnation as The Beach Boys."

✦✦✦✦

DEAN TORRENCE:

"Life without Surfin' USA would be like sex without girls!"

♦♦♦♦

"I'll say good-bye to my old hang-outs,
I want to see what The Beach Boys sing about".

—Lou Christie
from "Hollywood's My Stop", 1966

It's no less true in 1976 than in 1966. Ten years later the Beach Boys are still singing about the California good life. The minute you hear those harmonies brimming over with energy and enthusiasm (whether they're singing "Surfin", "Good Vibrations" or their new hit "Rock & Roll Music"), everything clicks—sun and sand, ears and guitars. You're California dreaming and you wish you were there. There's no way to count the number of kids over the years who've deserted their old stomping-grounds to check out what the Beach Boys were singing about.

But it's not just California. As time goes by (and especially lately, with their globe-spanning tours), The Beach Boys have come to mean

more. In their songs and stance, they represent what's great about America, on every level from summer fun-in-the-sun, to deeper themes like freedom and mobility, everything that's made America (for most of us, anyway) the greatest, youthful culture ever; Teenage Heaven on earth. And if the foregoing sounds excessively mawkish, can assure you that hearing the Beach Boys sing provokes a profounder patriotic thrill than that national anthem, "America the Beautiful," and Kate Smith put together. For their generation (the kids of the sixties and the seventies), The Beach Boys are America.

—Ken Barnes
June, 197?

The fourth annual
BRIAN WILSON & THE BEACH BOYS ISSUE.
May, 1973, August, 1974, July, 1975 June, 1976

AMERICA CELEBRATES THE BEACH BOYS

"This is Gonna be the Most Outrageous Summer Story of All" --Mike Love

By KEN BARNES

CALIFORNIA
HANG 9
SMALIBU?

He's not joshing, either. The Beach Boys are revving up for their biggest multi-media assault ever. And one of the media to be assaulted this time will be records -- *15 Big Ones*, the first new Beach Boys studio album since January 1973 and *Holland*, is completed and scheduled for early July release. An LP preview, their new single "Rock & Roll Music," the Chuck Berry/Beatles classic, is just out and already looks like a certified smash.

Added to their music of the day, the Beach Boys are planning their most extensive, most spectacular tour yet, one that should leave no stadium or major city unplayed.

They're set for their first network TV special, a nationally syndicated 15th Anniversary radio documentary that should blanket the country, plus projected cover stories in major news magazines (*Time* and *Newsweek* level), books, you name it. 15 years after their South Bay debut, the Beach Boys are preparing to make the biggest splash of their career.

The tour begins in July and lasts, off and on, till the end of the year. "The July 4th weekend...will probably be the biggest...ever in the group's history of touring," Mike Love told KMET/L.A. listeners during a stage-setting tribute. "The 1st and 2nd we'll be

in Oakland at the stadium there. Down here we'll be at Anaheim Stadium on the 3rd." Appearing with them will be Poco and America, both of whom just might come to regret the day they ever got on the same stage with the Beach Boys. "Then we just got an offer to go to Philadelphia to play a 90,000-seat stadium on July 4."

That last Bicentennially-apropos Philly date is confirmed, and should warm the hearts of the Beach Boys, who at one time wanted to be named the official Bicentennial band (feeling, rightly, that no one else represented American values quite so well). The first leg of the tour continues

till September 19, touching bases at most of the country's available stadium venues, and it's estimated the group will play before 1.2 million people during those 2 ½ months. They'll pick up again in the fall, until about 80 dates have been played in all, culminating in a New Year's Eve 1976-77 show which will mark their 15th performing anniversary.

The Beach Boys will be performing on a special set, which according to a spokesman is "a mock-up of a boat, with palm trees and twinkling lights to get the effect of water rippling along the sides. It's so complex we're taking two crews, one to set it up and

Beach Boys Influence: Not Just a Sound but a Lifestyle

By MARK SHIPPER

With a new album, a summer tour, and the return of a more-active Brian Wilson, it seems safe to say that the Beach Boys are definitely back. But it's also safe to say that they've never really been gone. In one form or another, the sound that Brian Wilson & Co. created fifteen years ago has seldom been off the charts. When the Eagles take off with their customary soaring harmonies, or Henry Gross sends chills up your spine with a song like "Shannon," you immediately realize that these records could not have existed had there been no Beach Boys.

Almost every major group has, at one time or another, paid tribute to the Beach Boys. The Who were one of the earliest to display overt Beach Boys' influence in songs like "Barbara Ann," and "Bucket T." Pete Townsend and Keith Moon particularly have never been reluctant to credit Brian Wilson for much of the Who's sound. (Moon, in fact, had a solo version of "Don't Worry Baby" out as a single last year). The opening track on the Beatles' White Album, "Back In The USSR," raised a few

eyebrows back in 1969 when first released. The song was loaded with obvious Beach Boys falsetto and 1969 (two years into "hip consciousness" and the denial of everything that came before it) was no time to dredge up the visions of hedonism that Beach Boys music always conveys. The Beatles, of course, were far removed from any kind of street sensitivity (thankfully) that would have prevented this song. Interestingly enough, "Back In The USSR" stands up, seven years later, better than anything else on that particular album.

There's something, some factor, in Beach Boys music that refuses to allow it to become dated. The most apparent evidence is the pair of Capitol re-issue albums that each went platinum last year. Capitol originally intended "Endless Summer" for the oldies market, aimed their TV advertising at it, and sat back in amazement at the phenomenal sales response from teenagers far too young to remember this music in its original release.

What is it about the Beach Boys that keeps their music contemporary when most other music from the mid-60's sounds every bit

of the ten years-old that it is? There's lots to be said for the abundance of social factors (girls, cars, and the beach are all still very much in vogue) but from a purely aural standpoint, a lot of credit has to go to Brian Wilson's production abilities. The sound achieved on pre-*Pet Sounds* albums like *Summer Days & Summer Nights* and *All Summer Long* is simply miles above anything else from the period, production-wise. And, an earlier record, "Don't Worry Baby," is so clean and contemporary that it seems more modern than the trio of re-makes (by Keith Moon, California Music, and Keller & Webb) that have appeared thus far in the seventies. Brian Wilson's mastery of the recording studio was every bit as complete as one of his idols, Phil Spector.

As for the social factors, the ideal life as expressed by Brian Wilson ten years ago (an endless summer of sunshine, cars, and girls) is still pretty much the idea for any kid with a chance at it today. When Eric Carmen delivered his most obvious Beach Boys tribute in "Drivin' Around," (from *Fresh*, the Raspberries second album) he covered it all: "Long hot

days/We'll be catchin' the rays/My tape deck is blastin'/My car's fast/I'm drivin' around...."* Carmen delved further on the final Raspberries album in "Cruisin' Music" and on his first solo LP with "Sunrise." More than any other contemporary artist, Carmen has used Brian Wilson as a source that can be returned to again and again.

Todd Rundgren is another artist who owns up to his Beach Boys debt. His carbon-copy "Good Vibrations" is on its way to being one of the few direct Beach Boy cover hits ever. Last summer's "Help Me Rhonda" by Johnny Rivers is another, but you have to go back over ten years for a third, "Little Honda" by the Hondells. While some may see this relative lack of cover-version success as an indication of something lacking in the material (there've been more than a dozen successful Beatle covers, for example) it's more likely due to the difficulty of out-doing (or even reaching) the original. It requires an artist with the pop skills of a Rundgren or Rivers to even approach it.

Rather than the almost-hopeless task of covering the Beach Boys, most seventies acts have chosen

(Cont'd. on Pg. 31)

15 BIG ONES
The Beach Boys
Brother/Reprise

By KEN BARNES

Last minute track-by-track first impressions of 15 BIG ONES: **Rock And Roll Music** [POPULARIZED BY CHUCK BERRY, THE BEATLES]: This one's familiar as a single already, but it makes a great leadoff track, too. Clever idea to cut it—renewing the Beach Boys' old Chuck Berry ties ["Surfin' USA" and half their early guitar intros] linking with the Beatles' inspired 1965 version. A timeless song anyway, unbeatable in 1957, 1965 or 1976. Full harmonies, Brian noticeably present and wailing, and Mike Love singing in his most Californian-nasal style, just like the old days. The natural sequel to "Surfin' USA" 13 years on, contemporized by drinking "beer from a wooden cup" instead of Berry's "home brew." Smash.

It's OK [WILSON-LOVE]: Amazing. Haven't heard the Beach Boys sound this summery since "Do It Again" in 1968. Short [2:18], lively, full production, it literally vaults out of the speakers. Definitely a premeditated [no TM puns intended] attempt to do it again [again], but it works better than I would have believed possible. New mature note of pessimism: "IT'S OK TO GO OUT AND HAVE SOME FUN.../IT'S OK, LET'S PLAY AND ENJOY IT WHILE IT LASTS..."

Had To Phone Ya [WILSON-LOVE]: Originally cut in 1973, but never released, by American Spring [Brian's wife Marilyn and her sister Diane]. An ethereal SUNFLOWER feel on a basically slight-but-pleasant song. Takes a few strange changes of direction, and ends with a Dennis Wilson vocal cameo.

Chapel Of Love [DIXIE CUPS, RONETTES]: This was always one of my least favorite Spector [and Greenwich-Barry] songs, but the Beach Boys translate it into a new dimension via a majestic all-stops-out production. About this point, most doubts about the course the Beach Boys' oldies bent would chart are disappearing. I'm still not sold on their CHOICE of material, but the execution seems impeccable.

Everyone's In Love With You [MIKE LOVE]: Mike's first solo composition [words & music] is a revelation. Swirling instrumental textures [Charles Lloyd on flute?] decorate an utterly irresistible melody. The Beach Boys haven't sounded this pretty since "Till I Die"[on SURF'S UP], but this is not a fearful, brooding mood piece but a lighthearted love ballad. Probably will emerge as my favorite track.

Talk To Me Talk To Me [LITTLE WILLIE JOHN SUNNY & THE SUNLINERS]: Sounds as good as could be expected, taking into account my lifelong personal aversion to the song. The PET SOUNDS-style bells and horn textures do wonders for the tune, but it still seems like a flatulent song warring with a delicate arrangement. A jarring interpolation of "Tallahassie Lassie" provides welcome, though fleeting, relief.

That Same Song [WILSON-LOVE]: A bouncy little trip through musicological history, very simple in conception but hard to resist. Brian's singing MUCH lower now; could hardly recognize him.

TM Song [BRIAN WILSON]: Starts boldly with a strident mock-argument recalling those "Cassius Love Vs. Sonny Wilson" studio goofs the Beach Boys used to mess around with to fill out their 1964 albums. Then a quiet voice announces "It's time for me to meditate," and we begin. Essentially a cosmic giggle, short [1:34], lightweight, and not overbearing in its spiritual advocacy. It wouldn't have sounded out of place on SMILEY SMILE but that was far from the best Beach Boys album.

Palisades Park [FREDDY CANNON]: Brian's reportedly been kicking this one around in his head for years. but it kicks off Side Two in fine fashion. A showpiece rearrangement turns frantic Freddy's roller coaster ride into a rhythmic rocker, with tasteful synthesizer fills and the patented full-to-bursting harmonies. For the second time on this album ["Chapel" was the first], they've transmuted teenage trivia into a majestic monument—and without smothering the original impulse of fun. Shades of "Amusement Park USA."

Susie Cincinnati [AL JARDINE]: This was the B-side of both "Add Some Music To Your Day" [1970] and the too-late-for-Christmas 1974 single "Child Of Winter," and although it's never been on an album, it's hard to understand what it's doing here six years after its first appearance. Maybe they wanted to give Al his big chance. It sounds fine, in any case, a sprightly story of a Cincinnati groupie ["city's #1 sinner"] on wheels.

A Casual Look [THE SIX TEENS FEATURING TRUDY WILLIAMS]: A hoary [1956] L.A. girl-group oldie, perhaps a little overnasalized in the lead vocals and played a bit too obviously for laughs, but once again it sounds great. The Beach Boys have a natural affinity for this sort of 50's doo-wop, as evidenced by the sharp a capella intro.

Blueberry Hill [FATS DOMINO]: As trite an oldie as you could dig up, it starts with an extended sax run and goes into a sparse string-bass-backed vocal. At this point it's the prime candidate for turkey of the set, but then it explodes into gear with that ever-electrifying neo-Spectorian Brian Wilson production in full riot. Just gets better and better, as they pull off another upset victory.

Back Home [BRIAN WILSON]: The only new original on Side Two spotlights Brian's new low voice again in a bucolic ditty about going back to the farm which doesn't particularly ring true. Pretty slight stuff, although the chorus picks up the momentum.

In The Still Of The Night [FIVE SATINS]: If there were ever a stale oldie you never wanted the Beach Boys to tackle, this was probably the one. But once again the production and background vocals are enough to rejuvenate the most jaded—another doo wop triumph. The lead singer [probably Brian] sounds extremely hoarse and uncharacteristically deep-voiced. A surprise stunner, here.

Just Once In My Life [RIGHTEOUS BROS.]: An unusual choice [surprising they didn't pick "You've Lost That Lovin' Feelin'," in keeping with the more obvious choices on the LP], and one I was looking forward to. Strangely, it's the only oldie here which doesn't quite come off, doubtless because the Phil Spector original was produced so brilliantly, and because no solo-singing Beach Boy can match Bill Medley on this one. There are moments of greatness, and the spectacular production pays homage to Spector while displaying subtle differences, but it ends up a valiant second best. The off-key singing [in spots] is disconcerting.

The vocals, in fact, are the one slight problem on 15 BIG ONES. The instrumental textures are appropriate, rich, and sumptuous, and the vocal harmonies are naturally unbeatable. But the lead vocals often sound excessively casual, as if the Beach Boys were trying too hard to prove they were having a good time in the studio.

That minor point aside, the album radiates an irrestible summershine kind of feeling, while at the same time displaying all the stunning production values Brian Wilson and the group are famous for. It's both awesome and relaxed, striking an inspired [and commercial] balance between the exuberance of their old records and the formalism of their recent efforts. It's got everything it needs, they're artists, and they do look back, but not in a spirit of blind fidelity to the original versions. Instead they turn the old songs into BEACH BOYS numbers, giving the album a unity rare in oldies-showcase projects. 15 BIG ONES is the album you've been hoping the Beach Boys would make for years now. It's a triumph.

No Beach Boys edition of Phonograph Record would be complete without Bruce Johnston [front, center]. Bruce has never forgotten how to have a good time—a firm believer in the future of fun.

to adapt their material to the sound. Henry Gross' "Shannon" is a prime example, and there have been scores of others, mostly less successful, chart-wise. Flash Cadillac's *Sons Of The Beaches* album from last year (on Private Stock) was thematically based on Beach Boys music, and one track, "Time Will Tell" perhaps comes the closest of anything recorded in the seventies to authentic Beach Boys standards. (Not close enough, unfortunately, to keep it from flopping dismally as a single last summer). For Beach Boys fans, though, this is required listening. Same goes for the Beverly Hills Blues Band, former Dino, Desi, & Billy stalwarts who've been fraternal with the Beach Boys ever since the demise of their original group. An album is coming this summer from Warner Brothers and expectations are high. Even more promising is Papa Do Ron Ron, a Southern California group under the wing of Dean Torrence. Their version of "Be True To Your School" (RCA) was a brilliant updating of the perennial classic. With an album in the works, a summer-full of gigs ahead, and the guidance of an acknowledged heavyweight in the field (Torrence), Papa Do Ron Ron, more than anyone else at this point, hold the promise of carrying the Beach Boys' torch into the future.

As for the present, there's never been more Beach Boys consciousness at any time in their career. It's gone beyond records into TV themes and even commercials (a sure signal of anything's contemporary appeal). The "Theme From Laverne & Shirley" by Cindi Greco is an unlikely marriage of girl group rock and vintage Beach Boys. Commercials like the current "Pepsi Generation" spot are full of solid Wilson references, and some even go further. Pay attention to

the backing track on this summer's Bonnie Bell suntan lotion commercial, and you'll hear a familiar tune that finally registers as "The Warmth Of The Sun" after a couple of listenings.

Clearly, after fifteen years, Beach Boys music is literally everywhere. When attempting to understand why, it's useful to consider this: there's something special and unique about music that is this *celebratory*. Far from the frustrated, misunderstood character that has dominated center-stage in rock & roll almost since the beginning, the Beach Boys (in their music) are having a great time and are thoroughly delighted to be right where they are. There'll always be a market for this sentiment. ("Suburban Soul Music," a friend calls it and that's about as apt a definition as you're likely to find). For every Bruce Springsteen hiding on the backstreets of Asbury Park, there are ten suburban kids hanging out at the new shopping center on a Saturday afternoon. Beach Boys music has always belonged to them. For another group to claim this audience, they'd not only have to be as talented as the Beach Boys, but they'd have to be as human and vulnerable, as well. Greil Marcus said it best in his excellent book, *Mystery Train* (E.P. Dutton, New York). "Unlike so many Hollywood groups that come from somewhere else," he writes, "the Beach Boys have never been fakes. They celebrated the freedom of California hedonism, looked for its limits, owned up to its failures, but never lost the ability to delight in the sun and to share that delight with others. Their pleasures, as opposed to those claimed by such seventies inheritors as the Eagles and America, have always radiated affection because those pleasures are rooted in friendship..."

In the end, it's been this "friendship," more than anything else, that's keeping old fans loyal and new ones coming. Pop Stars (which the Beach Boys have never appeared to be) go out of style. Friends don't. The Beach Boys won't.

* © 1973 CAM-USA Inc. (BMI)

KEN BARNES
(Cont'd. from pg. 27)
like a good, relaxed way to reinvolve Brian Wilson in the group's recorded affairs—his participation in the last three albums had been on the minimal side. The selected oldies apparently just popped out of Brian's head spontaneously; "That's what Brian was most comfortable doing," according to Dean. It was a good way for the entire group to test the waters again; they could just "get in and do it and have a good time. It's better than worrying about what they were going to do" (Dean

again). And, including the oldies is probably the best way to indicate to the public that the Beach Boys have recaptured the fun-first-and-foremost attitude that characterized their earlier material but was often absent on latter-day albums. *15 Big Ones* is a direct link to the Beach Boys' past, and as such it should have the broadest potential appeal to both old and new fans.

15 Big Ones is sure to be a smash hit, calibrated as it is with the opening of the group's tour. The TV, radio and magazine coverage will bolster the cause, and Warners is planning an all-out advertising/promotional blitz (as well they should), with TV spots galore. It's time to get ready. In 1961 the Beach Boys were "Surfin'." By 1963 they were "Surfin' USA." In 1976 they'll be celebrating Beach Boys USA, and it should be the biggest Beach Boys bash ever.

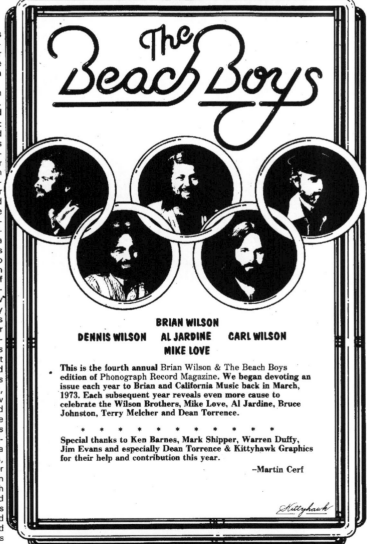

BRIAN WILSON
DENNIS WILSON   **AL JARDINE**   **CARL WILSON**
MIKE LOVE

This is the fourth annual Brian Wilson & The Beach Boys edition of Phonograph Record Magazine. We began devoting an issue each year to Brian and California Music back in March, 1973. Each subsequent year reveals even more cause to celebrate the Wilson Brothers, Mike Love, Al Jardine, Bruce Johnston, Terry Melcher and Dean Torrence.

*   *   *   *   *   *   *   *   *   *

Special thanks to Ken Barnes, Mark Shipper, Warren Duffy, Jim Evans and especially Dean Torrence & Kittyhawk Graphics for their help and contribution this year.

—Martin Cerf

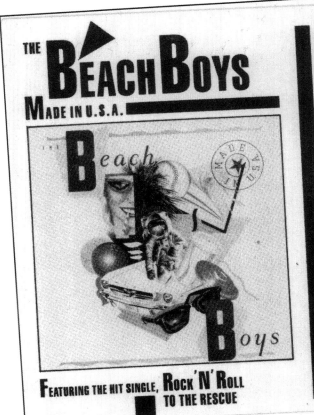

THE BEACH BOYS
MADE IN U.S.A.

FEATURING THE HIT SINGLE, Rock 'N' Roll TO THE RESCUE

25 YEARS
OF GREAT AMERICAN ROCK AND ROLL

SURFIN' SAFARI

409

SURFIN' U.S.A.

BE TRUE TO YOUR SCHOOL

SURFER GIRL

DANCE, DANCE, DANCE

FUN, FUN, FUN

I GET AROUND

HELP ME, RHONDA

DON'T WORRY BABY

CALIFORNIA GIRLS

WHEN I GROW UP (To Be A Man)

BARBARA ANN

GOOD VIBRATIONS

HEROES AND VILLAINS

WOULDN'T IT BE NICE

SLOOP JOHN B.

GOD ONLY KNOWS

CAROLINE, NO

DO IT AGAIN

ROCK AND ROLL MUSIC

COME GO WITH ME

GETCHA BACK

ROCK 'N' ROLL TO THE RESCUE

CALIFORNIA DREAMIN'

Capitol®
©1986 CAPITOL RECORDS, INC.

Radio ★ *Star*

THE BEACH BOYS
Cue Card #22

Today - Carl Wilson, Vocals - Guitar (B 12/26/46), Brian Wilson, Vocals - Bass, Keyboards (B 6-20-42), Mike Love - Vocals (B 3-15-41), Alan Jardine, Vocals -Guitar, (B 9-3-42), Bruce Johnston, Vocals -Keyboards (B 6-27-42) ★ Grew up in LA ★ Started as a family group ★ Brian, Carl & cousin Mike Love...Dennis not part of original group until mother made brothers let him join ★ Started as Carl & The Passions, became Kenny & The Cadets (Brian was Kenny) ★ Dennis was the only surfer... none of the other Beach Boys surfed...He persuaded them to do a song about the sport...Brian & Mike wrote "Surfin"...Father Murray was established songwriter...took them to his publisher...recorded on local "X" label... switched to Candix records ★ Group worked as Pendletones - Candix promotion man suggested name "Beach Boys" ★ Murray pursuaded Capitol Records producer, Nik Venet, to pick up group-first Capitol release, "Surfin Safari" went Top 20 ★ First LP - '63 "Surfin USA" went Gold-Had 8 Top 20 singles from '62 - '64-have had 24 Top 20 singles ★ Due to illness, Brian left in '65; replaced by Glen Campbell; Glen replaced by Bruce Johnston...Brian continued to oversee recording and be on stage when he wanted ★ Bruce Johnston wrote Barry Manilow's "I Write The Songs" ...Bruce is from Chicago ★ Beach Boys have 2 Gold singles - '66 "Good Vibrations" '64 "I Get Around" -Now released 27 LPs ★ Dennis died in a drowning accident in '83 group did not consider breaking up...had recording session on afternoon of press conference. ★ Sec. of Interior James Watt canceled Beach Boys performance in Washington, publicity was a real "Booster Shot" for their career ★ Still tour about a hundred dates a year-seasonally - do 27 songs a night but varies... have 350 songs in library 75% of shows are outside ★ Mike Love still a follower of transcendental meditation — meditates twice a day ★ Sunkist, which has had "Good Vibrations" as their theme for years, is sponsoring the Beach Boys 25th An-niversary tour this year - they will replace studio singers in Sunkist commercials ★ A new line of Sherry Holl/Beach Boys designed clothes called "Ho-Bo" has just hit the market.

© HNE Productions ★ P.O. Box 1168-594 ★ Studio City, CA 91604 ★ 213-871-0227

Please Place in CONTROL ROOM

The Beach Boys

HARRY LANGDON PHOTOGRAPHY © 1985

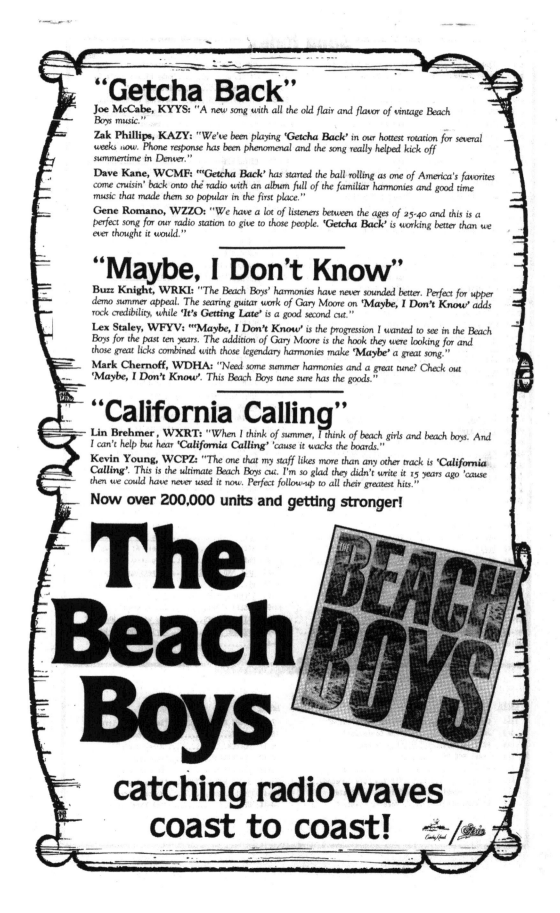

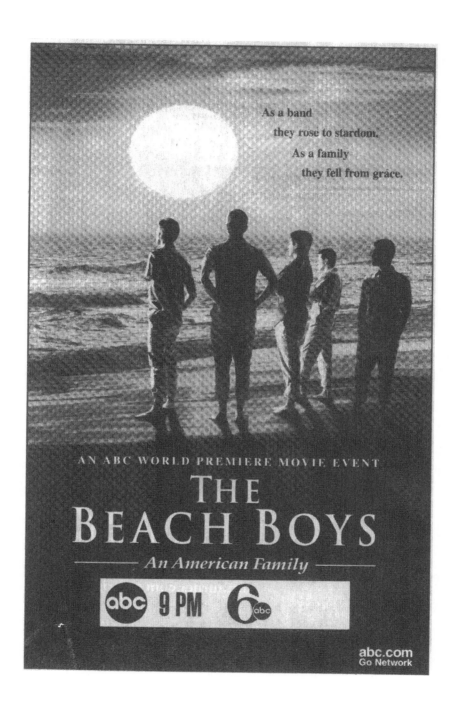

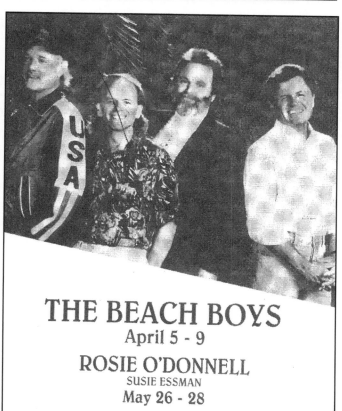

Capitol Records/Publicity Department
1750 North Vine Street, Hollywood, California 90028 (213) 462-6252

FOR IMMEDIATE RELEASE

NEWS:

CAPITOL TO RELEASE CLASSIC 1969
BEACH BOYS ALBUM LIVE IN LONDON

HOLLYWOOD, Nov. 10, 1976 - The Beach Boys Live In London,
which will be released Nov. 15, is the first new Beach Boys album
on Capitol Records besides repackages of already released material
since 1970, announces Jim Mazza, CRI Vice President, Marketing.

The album was recorded in 1969 and was released in England
in 1970. It became an immediate collector's item for many American
fans who searched for import copies. The record has never before
been released in the United States.

The Beach Boys perform a dozen tunes including many of their
best-known biggest hits, but concentrating on those that they made
popular during the mid to late sixties when they drifted away from the
surfing and hotrodding crazes and sang more about love and "good vibes".

The hits included reach back to "California Girls". Other
singles are "Barbara Ann", "God Only Knows", "Good Vibrations",
"Sloop John B", "Darlin' "and "Do It Again". "Wouldn't It Be Nice",
originally a flip side of one of their early singles as a studio version
and one of their most-requested concert numbers during this period,
is part of the package. There also are several non-original numbers
such as Bobby (he wrote "Route 66") Troup's "Their Hearts Were Full Of
Spring".

When The Beach Boys were recorded during this concert, they
were in prime form with their sparkling arrangements and legendary,
multi-voiced, layered harmonies in full evidence.

"We expect strong sales with this album," says Mazza. "The
Beach Boys' fans have been clamoring for more material from that era.

Capitol®

More

This album captures the group at the pinnacle of their career. It has sold extemely well in England since its release there. It's one of those classics that was previously overlooked in the release schedule here."

The Beach Boys early material remains immensely popular both here and abroad. In fact, a repackage released in England titled 20 Golden Greats followed in the amazing sales pattern set by the American-released Endless Summer and Spirit of America. During the past quarter of the fiscal year, the English record was the top-selling album there with an estimated three times the number of sales as its nearest competitor.

##

The 1984 Temple Owls

Invite you to

Say goodbye to summer with
TEMPLE OWL FOOTBALL
and
THE BEACH BOYS

Sept. 22
Temple vs. Pitt AND "The Beach Boys"

Philadelphia's Only Major College Football

Temple Season Tickets bring you this and much, much more in '84!

126

The Beach Boys The Pet Sounds Sessions
Produced By Brian Wilson

"No one is musically educated until they have heard PET SOUNDS... It was my inspiration for writing SGT. PEPPER."

Paul McCartney

The Beach Boys The Pet Sounds Sessions
Produced By Brian Wilson

THE 4-CD BOX SET FEATURING:
- The first ever true stereo mix of the album
- All of the symphonic instrumental backing tracks without vocals
- All of the choral-like vocals without instrumental backing tracks
- More than a dozen alternate versions of tracks from the sessions
- New 1997 HDCD sound technology, including the original mono album and "Good Vibrations"
- A 42-page full-color booklet with rare and unseen photos from the zoo session
- A 128-page book featuring exclusive interviews with the Beach Boys, George Martin, and Paul McCartney

Available November 4, 1997
At Record Stores Everywhere,
or Call 1.800.994.4455 to Order Now!

EMI-CAPITOL

©1997 Capitol Records, Inc. Printed In USA

Capitol RECORDS

128

MEDIA INFORMATION

FOR IMMEDIATE RELEASE
August 20, 1997

THE PET SOUNDS SESSIONS SET FOR RELEASE
ON CAPITOL/EPROP ON NOVEMBER 4
* Four Disc Box Set Celebrates Landmark Beach Boys LP *

"Nobody is educated musically until they've heard Pet Sounds...It is a
total classic record that is unbeatable in many ways."
- Paul McCartney

"Without Pet Sounds, Sgt. Pepper wouldn't have happened...
Pepper was an attempt to equal Pet Sounds."
- George Martin

On November 4, Capitol Records/EMI-Capitol Entertainment Properties will
release the long awaited THE BEACH BOYS The Pet Sounds Sessions, a four
disc audio "documentary" of one of the most enduring and influential
albums in the history of pop music.

Featuring previously unreleased alternative mixes, session highlights in
stereo, vocal and instrumental-only versions of the original album, a
first-ever stereo mix of Pet Sounds supervised by Brian Wilson, and a
remastered mono version of the album using "state-of-the-art" HDCD
technology, The Pet Sounds Sessions offers new insights into the
conception and creation of this classic work.

Hailed by critics and such artists as Paul McCartney, Elton John and Tom
Petty as perhaps the best pop album ever, Pet Sounds captured a moment
when The Beach Boys helped to transform pop music from a singles-driven
form of entertainment to an album-based form of communication. The Pet
Sounds Sessions allows the listener to experience the creative process
that fueled this metamorphosis and offers new justification for the
legion of fans and critics who long-ago realized Brian Wilson's genius
as a songwriter, arranger, composer, and producer.

From such seminal rockers as Lou Reed, John Cale, Todd Rundgren and Alex
Chilton to alternative superstars like R.E.M., Oasis, Tears For Fears
and Sonic Youth, the list of artists who have been influenced by Pet
Sounds is long and varied. The Beatles themselves have graciously cited
the album as a key inspiration for their Sgt. Pepper's Lonely Hearts
Club Band masterwork.

The best demonstration of The Beach Boys astounding artistic development
in this period can be heard in the deconstructed vocal and instrumental
tracks on this compilation. For the first time, the soaring and
intricate harmonies that are the Beach Boys trademark can be fully
appreciated. Playing like modern-day Gregorian chant, the mesmerizing
vocal-only cuts highlight the spiritual aspect of the songs with
arrangements that convey the sense of love and longing that lies at the
conceptual heart of the album. "Wouldn't It Be Nice," "You Still
Believe In Me" and "God Only Knows" are breathtaking examples of the
Beach Boys pure skills as singers.

     EMI-CAPITOL ENTERTAINMENT PROPERTIES

5750 WILSHIRE BOULEVARD, SUITE 300, LOS ANGELES, CA 90036 • TEL 213 692-1100 FAX 213 692-1295

Alternately, the instrumental-only tracks and session highlights can clearly be heard as a "mini-symphony," with the chamber-ish "string-only" arrangement for **"Don't Talk"** being the most striking example. The orchestral feel of the arrangements is due, in large part, to Brian's drafting an army of session players for the songs and his use of musical instruments not traditionally found in pop recordings at the time. One of the real treats of this compilation is actually hearing -- for the first time in stereo -- the variety of instruments involved, and how so many seemingly disparate sounds mesh so naturally. From sleigh bells to theremin, church organ to banjo, the complexity of the compositions and the simplicity and directness of their appeal is just magical. The fact that Brian was able to make the whole dense brew rock is another achievement entirely.

In addition to the incredible vocal and instrumental tracks, a few of the rarities unearthed by Brian Wilson and co-producers **Mark Linett** and **David Leaf** include a version of **"God Only Knows"** with sax solo on the bridge, Brian singing the entire lead on **"God Only Knows"** and **"Sloop John B,"** **"Hang On To Your Ego"** with original lyrics, Brian's original piano demo for **"Don't Talk (Put Your Head On My Shoulder)"** and the original version of **"Caroline, No"** presented in the key and tempo in which it was actually recorded. Bonus songs include **"Trombone Dixie"** -- horn arrangements recorded at sessions just prior to the Pet Sounds period -- and an excerpt of the first recording of **"Good Vibrations,"** a song started, but never completed, during the album sessions.

A comprehensive introduction and historical essay, complete session musician interviews, track-by-track and disc-by-disc production notes written and compiled by Beach Boys historian David Leaf, add perspective to the musical achievement. An additional 120 page CD-sized book features extensive comments from Brian Wilson and his chief 'competitors' (Paul McCartney, George Martin), collaborators (Pet Sounds lyricist Tony Asher, Beach Boys) and other engineers and musicians who created this landmark recording.

# # #

CONTACT: Sujata Murthy @ EPROP 213-692-1117

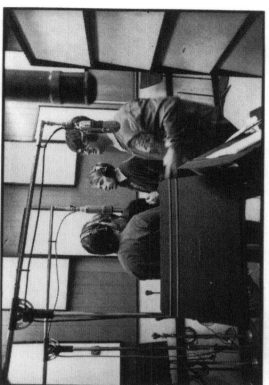

L-R) Bruce Johnston, Carl Wilson, Al Jardine, Dennis Wilson, Mike Love

L-R) Carl Wilson, Dennis Wilson, Al Jardine, Brian Wilson

The Beach Boys
The Pet Sounds Sessions

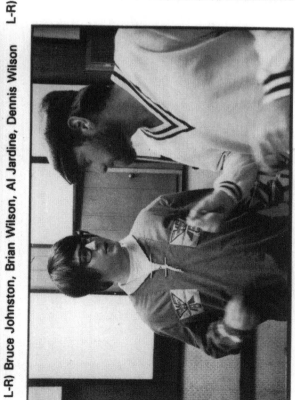

L-R) Bruce Johnston, Brian Wilson, Al Jardine, Dennis Wilson

L-R) Brian Wilson, Mike Love

EMI-CAPITOL
ENTERTAINMENT PROPERTIES

EMI-CAPITOL
ENTERTAINMENT PROPERTIES

BRIAN WILSON

The
Beach Boys
The Pet Sounds Sessions

It's been fun, fun, fun.

Thank you,
Alan, Brian, Carl, Dennis and Mike

The Beach Boys

SALISBURY/METTER

Dear Brian, Carl, Michael, Alan and Dennis:

I want to take this opportunity to make a personal statement about how proud I am to have had the privilege of working with you these past seven years.

I can sincerely say that devoting my exclusive energies to the furtherance of your careers has been a richly satisfying professional cause.

As the activities of this year unfold, know that these events are the culmination of the hopes and hard work of the many good and loyal people who have supported you so steadfastly in recent years.

On behalf of all of us who wish you well, thank you for past memories and for that which is yet to come.

With continued affection,

Stephen Love

Thank you for
Fifteen Great Ones

washington
rock concert
magazine ™

JUNE/JULY 1979
$1.00 UK 60P

THE BEACH BOYS

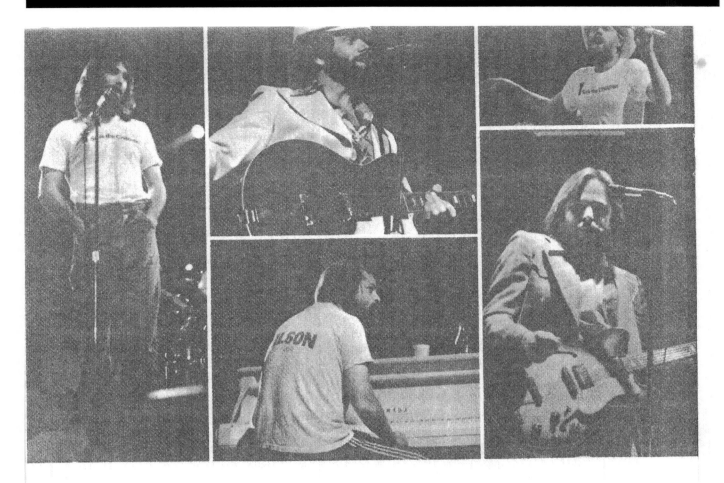

THE BEACH BOYS

by Harry Sumrall

Photos/David Werth

Mike Love

THE WORD IS OUT ... about the Beach Boys ... the word *has* been out for years.

"You don't want to talk to Michael and Dennis together. One of them will get mad and storm out of the room."

"No group interviews on the way to the show. They are taking separate limos."

"The last time Brian was interviewed, he refused to say anything."

"Don't mention the disco single to Dennis. He gets very angry about disco."

"Alan never has much to say."

"Carl will talk, but he is very sensitive about the press."

The press knows it. The public knows it. Even the tour entourage knows it. All is not sun and fun in the Wilson clan. Madness, conflicts, tantrums, drugs — the dark images titillate the imagination, especially when they are set against the brightness of the music and the glow of youth that envelopes the group.

In the personality-oriented, plastic seriousness of the late 70s, the Beach Boys have become the number one soap opera of prime time rock 'n' roll. Their off stage exploits receive as much attention as their on stage performances. Every writer/amateur analyst has written a pithy Beach Boy tract. Every fan has a favorite story about Brian's neurosis. The Beach Boys are like a small town scandal — their music may be enjoyable, but their problems are "fun, fun, fun."

The group itself seems to be as fascinated by its notoriety as the public. In a twisted way they seem as caught up in the friction as everyone else. They are always ready with an incendiary quote. There is always a dispute, just when attention starts to flag. Even their reactions to the reactions reinforce the atmosphere of compulsive hostility. Brian is reclusive. Alan is shy and retiring. Mike retreats into mysticism. Dennis parades his uninhibited lifestyle like a lusty evangelist. Carl is obsessively indifferent.

"There's elements of sibling rivalries, outright arguments and flare-ups," ex-

plains Michael Love, "but the juxtaposition of personalities also creates a dynamic." Michael Love has an ingenious way of qualifying himself that must have produced many of the nasty quotes attributed to him. He says things like, "Brian has a problem coping with society, but he is all right on a one to one basis," or "He's [Brian] not really cultured and refined, however, he is very intelligent about music." Take away the second portions of those statements and you have a searing Love interview.

He is self-consciously serious and intellectual. He talks constantly throwing out 25 cent words like verbal confetti. "I meditate assiduously," he says, drawing out the "siduously" like a piece of taffy. When it is suggested that he, more than anyone, has provided the ammunition for journalistic cannons, he shrugs, "I am the most gregarious. The others can't verbalize themselves as well as I."

About the problems, he explains, "It's no secret that Dennis and I have different ideas about the approach to life." He says this quietly, with over-stated understatement. Then, the tense laugh of a

Al Jardine

used car salesman, "Obviously, the Beach Boys do not meet after every show at an ice cream parlor."

Carl Wilson has a different approach. In recent years, he has assumed the unofficial leadership of the group and it has been said that his even temperament has kept the group together. He is impassive; his guard, constantly up. Somehow his reticence is much more disturbing than Love's verbiage. When difficulties are mentioned, he withdraws. "In every family there is unpleasantness. Anyway, I never read any press about the Beach Boys."

Alan Jardine is the exception to the Beach Boy rule. The only non-Wilson (Love is a first cousin), he has an objectivity that is engaging when compared to the forced personalities of the rest of the group. "There's been a lot of self-indulgence in the group, a lack of discipline. The self-indulgent thing happens when money happens," he says, matter-of-factly. "We only started out to do one record, and now here we are 17 years later. It was fun for about a year, then it wasn't 'fun, fun, fun,' anymore."

He attributes many of the group's highly publicized problems to their early success and the pressures that were created by that success. "When you have a hit record, the businessmen are swimming around you like white sharks and you are their next meal," he says. The record business, he believes, has affected many young musicians badly, financially and personally. He states with a certain disdain, "You have no idea what's in store for you."

After all the hyperbole from the press, the fans, the entourage and the group, Jardine's realistic view is something of a jolt. He sees the Beach Boys merely as a group and a family and leaves it at that.

The emotional and psychological garbage is left in the can. Small wonder that he doesn't get the same amount of attention as the rest of the boys. *Doesn't Alan realize that he just isn't playing the game?*

THE WORD IS OUT . . . about the Beach Boy's music . . . and that word is "Art."

"Well, why not, it's a great legend, and just like nearly everything the Beach Boys ever recorded, I can never stop listening to it. [the lp, "15 BIG ONES".] Mainly it's about Brian Wilson . . . who tuned his one good ear into the drone of middle-class America and heard the lost chord of God."

Rolling Stone
November 4, 1976

At one time in the early years it was actually possible to *enjoy* a Beach Boys' record. Kids danced to their music at parties. The songs were like teenage muzak that was played in every record store, surf shop and hamburger joint in the country. Guys kept track of their favorite dates with Beach Boys' songs. Let's see, Alice was "I Get Around," Linda was "Little Deuce Coup," Veronica was "Shut Down." The Beach Boys were a "pop" group in the most basic sense — their music was so popular that it became the soundtrack for virtually every teen activity.

Suddenly the pop market changed. The Beatles added strings and sitars to their music. The Who was labelled Pop-Art Rock. Dylan became an "important poet." Pop music became serious. Songwriters were referred to as composers. Soon it was impossible for any self-respecting rock fan to buy a Beach Boys' record without feeling culturally inferior.

That's when Brian Wilson became a genius. The Beach Boys released the single "Good Vibrations" which sent critics stumbling over themselves clamoring for superlatives. College students wrote insightful essays. The lp *Pet Sounds* sent further shivers up the artistic spines of the Rock intelligentsia. The Beach Boys were transformed from five happy-go-lucky beach bums into the "voices of a generation." Books were written comparing them to everyone from Bach to Beethoven.

"They'll be playing our music four hundred years from now, as a music that exemplified a whole society," Michael Love states in his own gregarious way. If that's a bit strong, like saying Dagwood Bumstead represents the 20th century work ethic, it's not any worse than the proclamations of the press and the public. A publicity sheet exclaims that "if Brian had lived in another century he might well have been picking out parts to

Dennis Wilson

Photos/David Werth

Beethoven sonatas on his piano after school."

Pet Sounds, however, marked the apex of their creative work. Increasingly, the group has returned in recent years to their earlier sound. Despite this trend, the "genius syndrome" has persisted and the older songs have been reinterpreted to conform to this attitude. After all, those songs about "Surfin' Safaris" and hot rods were really "timeless evocations of the joys of youth," weren't they? Love sums up by saying, "There will always be a Beach Boys, even after we have all left this planet."

Carl is slightly more down to earth. "I think the music is a 'feel'; I think it 'feels' more than it 'says'." Asked if the group's newest single "Good Timin' " is a throwback to early days, Carl is noncommittal. "I don't know about the record sounding like the surf songs, its just Beach Boy music; it's the way we sound."

The record is similar to the group's "old" style with a warm melody line and splendid harmonies that amble along effortlessly. Yet, the ad for the *L.A. Light* album features a hushed voice intoning "Brian . . . Dennis . . . Carl . . . Mike . . . Al . . . The genius of the Beach Boys."

The artistic hype nonwithstanding, it is still the oldies that keep the group going. While their records sell at a moderate rate (the disco single "Here Comes the Night" reached number 45 on the charts) the Beach Boys' concerts consistently sell out major arenas. The reason — their set is dominated by the oldies.

"I think you get a little crotchety after awhile," jokes Alan, about playing the songs for the thousandth time. He is just as whimsical about the importance of their music, "Some of them [the songs] of course, are tedious, but you get to appreciate them like old friends." As if to diffuse the artistic babblings of the group and its public, he defends the simplicity of the oldies, "Why pretend that you hate them? If it wasn't for us, they wouldn't be here, and if it wasn't for them, we wouldn't be here."

No artistic pretentions, no posturing — This guy just isn't very much fun at all, is he?

THE WORD IS OUT about Brian Wilson . . . and the word isn't good.

"Brian isn't doing any talking on this tour."

"If you see Brian, please don't go near him."

"Whatever you do, don't say anything to Brian."

The voice always lowers a bit, the eyes narrow, a smirk suggests, "Let's not make waves."

Whether spoken by tour managers, publicists or record company reps, the feeling is the same. Everyone is *very* concerned about Brian Wilson.

continued

Brian Wilson

Carl Wilson

When Brian appears, first in the lobby of the Watergate Hotel and later, back-stage at the Capital Centre, he seems remote, but in a nonchalant sort of way. He strolls about in wrinkled jogging pants and a green T-shirt, grasping a bottle of Coke and staring absent-mindedly at the carefully distant crowd around him. There is the uneasy feeling that he must be thinking, "Why doesn't anyone talk to me?"

Brian Wilson has some serious emotional problems. If you don't believe it, just ask any fan, writer, or confidant. The tales of his behavior, of course, are usually accompanied either by sorrowful nods or mischievious chuckles, depending on the character of the character who's doing the telling. Brian Wilson has become rock's weird uncle who everyone keeps locked up in the attic . . . and then talks about.

Everyone gets mileage out of Brian's problems. The rock press is never without good copy, as long as they have a resident, raving genius on their hands ("That story about the sandbox in Brian's house was cute," says Michael Love, sarcastically). The public loves a juicy bit of gossip about Brian. The Beach Boys themselves haven't been hurt by the reputation of their tormented genius. And, while the two psychiatrists who accompany him on tour, surely provide him

with a lot of support, at a reported $90 an hour, they are being supported pretty well themselves.

Brian has certainly been true to his group. His early compositions defined their style and sound ("90% of the musical juggernaut to 'Wild Honey' was Brian," states Love) and his more complex work established the artistic standing which helped them survive the lean years when they were not as popular as they are now. "As long as Brian is in the picture," says Alan, "there will always be that leadership."

In fact, many of Brian's problems began when he went from being a "competent songwriter" to a "genius." Love believes the possibility of being a genius was "much too much for him to handle." He says that, "before he was messed up, he was innocent, almost to the point of buffoonery. I don't think he was balanced enough to handle it. You're dealing with a guy who has been told in his early life by his father, that he didn't know what he was doing. Emotionally, this was very confusing when everyone told him how talented he was."

No one seems to know the extent of Brian's "madness." Some suggest the breakdowns are ruses to avoid the stickiness of business and personal conflicts within the group. Others believe he is so obsessed with his music that his mind

Photos: David Werth

cannot deal with practical, day-to-day existence.

The fact of Brians behavior is sad enough. What is most depressing, however, is the way in which his personal problems have been pounced upon by literally everyone. The press and the fans have been bad, but the Beach Boys themselves are no winners either. Somewhere in Santa Monica, one suspects, there is a warehouse full of "Brian is Back" posters, waiting for the next tour.

Alan states simply, "Brian parented the group, now, we are parenting him." *With an objective attitude like that, Al could really get to be a bore.*

THE WORD IS OUT about a Beach Boys' concert . . . No word is needed.
"In this summer's almost SRO tour, the Beach Boys are reaching audiences from 40 to 15."
— People Magazine

Brilliant spotlights illuminate the white stage with its white backdrops, white amplifiers, white piano, white everything. The crowd waits before the spectacle like a group of wondrous terrestrials gazing in awe at a benevolent mother ship. A Strauss waltz ("We ran out of downers," quips producer Bruce Johnston, backstage) adds a light, festive musical atmosphere and the scene has the wholesome air of a country picnic.

The lights are lowered. A hush. Then, there they are! The Beach Boys rush onto the stage and launch into "California Girls." Screams. Everyone is on their feet, dancing, swaying to the music. The songs leap from the speakers. A mass of voices sings the familiar words along with the group like a mammoth, out of tune chorus. Al catches a swimming tube that is hurled to the stage. Mike kicks a brightly colored beach ball into the crowd. Dennis dances on the piano. Carl stands, rooted, at the front of the stage. Brian sits quietly behind his piano, an occasional smile acknowledging the response. Each song is greeted with an ovation louder than the one before. At the end of the show, lights arc across the crowd, momentarily illuminating middle-aged marrieds, long-haired teens and bouncing children — three generations of Beach Boy addicts who are hooked on the boisterous highs of the music.

The concert brings everything into perspective. The preoccupation with problems, the artistic pretensions, the mental state of Brian Wilson become adolescent dabblings which are overshadowed by the sheer pleasure which the music brings to the crowd. Alan is probably right when he says, "Sometimes I feel like an extended teenager, locked in a time warp of teenagedom." When it comes to the Beach Boys.

PET Sounds

Stereo gear for your room, your little deuce coupe or your sloop *John B.*

Wouldn't it be nice to own all this bitchin' stereo equipment? Wouldn't it be nice to be rich? You're not going to make any money if you spend all your time surfing, so get out of the water, cruise for burgers and listen to the Beach Boys on these neat car stereos and accessories:

1. *Jensen C-9991 3-Way Triaxial® Speaker System (4" X10"), $119.95;* **2.** *Metro Sound Ultra-Fi MS-7600 AM/FM Stereo w/ cassette player. $259.95;* **3.** *Clarion PE-662C AM/FM Stereo Tuner w/automatic reverse cassette ($269.95), Clarion SK-99 Speaker System ($129.95 per pair), and Clarion 300 EQB Graphic Equalizer/Power Booster ($169.95);* **4.** *Jensen C9999 In-door Triaxial® Speaker System w/high-frequency module and 5¼" woofer, $117.95;* **5.** *Akai SW-7 Mini-Speakers (for car* *or home), $145 per pair;* **6.** *Sanyo FT-1670 AM/FM/Cassette w/ built-in power amp, digital clock w/elapsed timer and automatic radio signal scanning. $369.95;* **7.** *Jensen R-330 AM/FM/8-Track w/separate R-330 Power Amp. $469.95;* **8.** *Craig T-633 AM/FM/Cassette. $199.95;* **9.** *Jensen J-1001 Separates System w/two 6"X9" woofers, two mid-range speakers and two tweeters plus handy control unit (it's sitting atop the R-330), $189.95. Now, climb out of the car and turn the page.*

January 1979 Chic 79

148

Receivers

Even if you weren't made for these times, these receivers and phones were made for you: 1. Koss PRO AAA Headphones, $75; 2. the State-of-the-Art Marantz 2600 AM/FM Stereo Receiver with 300 watts per channel into 8ohm speakers (400 into 4). $1600; 3. a stately Sansui G-6000 AM/FM Stereo Receiver with lots of buttons $630; 4. the space-age JVC JR-S301 AM/FM Stereo Receiver which includes a built-in graphic equalizer, $479; 5. KLH Burwen Research PRO-8 Headphones, $115; 6. a nifty Nikko NR-615 AM/FM Stereo Receiver, a mere $270; 7. the Kenwood KR-8010 AM/FM Stereo Receiver, packing a potent 125 watts per channel, $675.

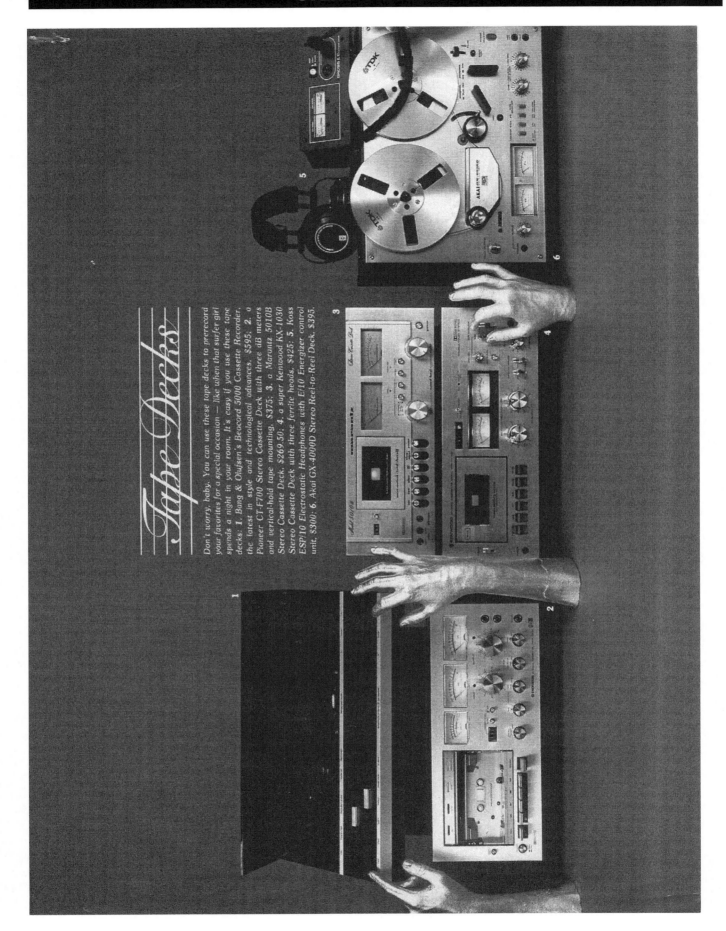

Tape Decks

Don't worry, baby. You can use these tape decks to prerecord your favorites for a special occasion — like when that surfer girl spends a night in your room. It's easy if you use these tape decks. 1. Bang & Olufsen's Beocord 5000 Cassette Recorder, the latest in style and technological advances, $595; 2. a Pioneer CT-F700 Stereo Cassette Deck with three dB meters and vertical-hold tape mounting, $375; 3. a Marantz 5010B Stereo Cassette Deck, $269.50; 4. a super Kenwood KX-1030 Stereo Cassette Deck with three ferrite heads, $425; 5. Koss ESP/10 Electrostatic Headphones with E/10 Energizer control unit, $300; 6. Akai GX-4000D Stereo Reel-to-Reel Deck, $395.

Photographed by James Baes

Speaker Systems

Your lust has overcome you, but Caroline says no. Drown out her protestations with these fine speaker systems: 1. ESS Inc.'s AMT-1B Heil air-motion transformer loudspeaker (looks strange, works like a miracle), $488 each; 2. Koss CM-1020 3-way Speaker System in a cabinet whose beauty must be seen to be appreciated, $325 each; 3. the Jensen LS-5 3-way Speaker System, $219.95 each; 4. Cerwin-Vega S-1 Bookshelf Speakers (system includes a nifty gadget — not shown — called a Bass Evacuator to uncover low frequencies), $450 each; 5. Altec Model Seven Series II, $259 each. Prices on all equipment are manufacturer's suggested retail, and units can often be had for less at your local stereo dealer. Hey, we've got stores all over . . . so come on down! □

3   4   5

PERSONALITY PROFILE

special guest
FIREFALL

TUESDAY JUNE 14 - 8PM

Summer just wouldn't be Summer without
the Beach Boys and on Flag Day, June 14th
they'll shower that California sunshine
on the Mann Music Center.

The Beach Boys are comprised of brothers
Brian, Carl and Dennis Wilson, cousin
Mike Love and friends Al Jardine and Bruce
Johnston. Their upbeat songs and contagious
harmonies have been entertaining fans for
22 years. With the same lineup intact,
the Beach Boys own the enviable distinction
of being the longest running original
member band in rock'n'roll history.

In 1961 they produced "Surfin," a tune that
would singlehandedly create the "California
Sound" of the early 60's. And now in 1983,
after 35 albums, 14 of them gold. the Beach
Boys continue to brighten the airwaves with
references to sun, sand and surf as well
as those "California Girls."

This summer they embark on their longest
tour in 21 years, playing capacity audiences
from May through September, highlighted
by 52,000 fans at Jack Murphy Stadium in
San Diego in early May.

It was only two summers ago when the Beach
Boys put on their biggest beach party yet.
They played to more than 500,000 fans at
the foot of the Washington Monument on
July 4th, followed by another record setting
crowd the next day at the Queen Mary in
Long Beach, California. The latter show
was nationally broadcasted live on an FM
simulcast.

The Beach Boys saga had its beginning in
Hawthorne, California in 1961. The Wilson's
were a musical family, mother Audrey played
the organ and father Murry never lost sight
of his songwriter aspirations. The three

brothers would routinely harmonize together
in their room.
Brian loved the Four Freshman and Chuck
Berry, spending hours at the piano picking
out parts of songs. He'd take the high
part, giving the bass line to Mike, the
baritone to Dennis and Carl the tenor.
Jardine, a folk music fan was a teammate
of Brian's on the Hawthorne High School
football team and was invited to join the
group.

Dennis was the only surfer in the group
and noticing the surfing craze unfold,
talked Brian, Carl and Mike into writing
a song about it. By December of 1961,
the group, under the name the Beach Boys
had recorded their first record, "Surfin',"
on the small Candix label which became a
regional hit.

The group signed to Capitol Records in
1962 under the management of father Murry,
with their first national release, "409"
and "Surfin' Safari," which became a
doublesided top 10 hit.

The Beach Boys remained in high gear as
the top ten hits continued with "Surfin'
U.S.A.," "Shut Down," "Surfer Girl," "Little
Deuce Coup," "Fun, Fun, Fun," "I Get
Around," "Don't Worry Baby," "California
Girls" and "Help Me Rhonda." Between 1963
and 1964, the group's records never left
the charts including seven consecutive
top 10 singles.

Soon afterwards the intense recording and
concert schedule began to take it's toll
on Brian. It was at this time that the
ballads and Mike Love's mid-range vocals
were featured on the rockers.

Glen Campbell joined the road show in 1965,
but was later replaced by Bruce Johnston
who remains in the band today.

Over the years the Beach Boys have continued
to produce hit after hit. Their music
remains timeless, uplifting and positive,
as summed up by Dennis Wilson, "People use
the Beach Boys for what they think America
should be. The Beach Boys created a safe
place for People."

STEVE KAHN'S

SUPERSCENE™

A SUMMER CONTEST BY THE GROUP WHICH INVENTED SUMMER!

If The Beach Boys didn't invent summer, then who did? For 18 years now, the group's "good vibrations" have captured California's sunshine in words and music!

Brian Wilson, Mike Love, Al Jardine, Carl Wilson and Dennis Wilson have gotten older over the years — and, as the commercial says, better!

An exciting new book — "The Beach Boys, The Authorized Biography of America's Greatest Rock and Roll Band!" — has just been published by Ballantine Books. It's a big and beautiful book, jammed with color pictures and posters! And it can be yours!

All you've got to do is make at least three words out of "The Beach Boys." It's as easy as that (hey, it's the middle of August and we're all into lazy, hazy days, so why shouldn't this week's contest be easy?).

There's one guaranteed winner among the readers of this newspaper, who will be selected in a random drawing.

Enter today! It's a contest with "good vibrations!"

THE BEACH BOYS

_____

_____

_____

Mail To: Beach Boys SuperScene Contest c/o This Newspaper

I've made three words out of "The Beach Boys":

Name _____ Age _____

Address _____

City _____ State/Province _____ Zip _____

My School _____ My Phone No. _____

(Please Mail By Friday)

©1979 by The Keasy Corporation
Dist. by NYT Special Features
8/12

For a Dollar and an Old Surfin' Safari LP, We'll Send You a Dry New Reprise LP by (Believe It) 1971's Beach Boys -- Surf's Up.

The Beach Boys? 1971? Surf's Up?

Yes, here it is nearly 10 years after the birth of America's Most Indigenous Rock and Roll Group, a decade during which the Beach Boys have defined and refined a distinctive brand of music with experiments which began in the marketplace and have ended practically in a museum.

The Problem Unveiled

Exulting critics have replaced screaming crowds in that time, and in that museumful of exultant critics lies The Beach Boys' and Reprise's problem. There are very few real live people left in the room.

The Beach Boys and their current music deserve a real big audience of real live people and an arena at least the size of the Mojave Desert.

Thus, Reprise Records (this time conjugally with Brother Records) once again goes to its knees with an offer (valid only in 1971; from '72 on, Warner/Reprise will stop this foolishness) that is absurdly generous. Also, one hopes, apt.

Doomed by Name

It is Reprise/Brother Records' feeling that—by their name alone—The Beach Boys are doomed in today's record market. To E. J. of Topeka, Kansas, The Beach Boys are still ridin' the surf off Malibu.

So there's a mighty PR (public relations) job to do, 'specially when you consider that the BBs not only are on a salt-water-free diet but also:

▪ have just recorded an epic new album which is already garnering those dreaded critical raves

▪ have confusingly titled that album not something really acceptable like Spaced Heavies but instead with an image throwback, Surf's Up. Surf's Up? Yes, Surf's Up

▪ have been playing at places with nary a speck of sand, like Washington's March for Peace and fund-raisers for the Berrigan Brothers

▪ recently joined The Grateful Dead in a midnight jam at The Fillmore East which held everybody, including Bob Dylan, enthralled

▪ have accomplished this social and musical metamorphosis without betraying the harmonic and rhythmic strengths their music has always boasted

▪ have accomplished this s&m metamorphosis without acknowledgment from you masses out there.

Greedy? Sure.

So, any fool can plainly see why Brother/Reprise is ever-so-momentarily relaxing its normal greedy stance: a massive PR job is underway to convince the Northern Hemisphere that the BBoys can once again be called your contemporaries.

To do so, we are trying to rid this whole world of the old Capitol surfin' albums. To start, Reprise is offering the Beach Boys new Surf's Up album in exchange for a dollar and your used copy of Surfin' Safari (Capitol T-1808). The fine points of this offer are nailed down in yonder coupon's fine type.

Best of All, Though,

is our assumption that not many of those old Capitol creakers still exist.

So that, to get Surf's Up, you'll have to buy it regular.

This, to those turned rabid by this ad, will mean a heavier investment. A search of shops for the new Surf's Up. For Reprise and Brother is, thank the Lord, also able to offer copies of this best new BBoys album to those who need to pay retail.

It is available in department stores, discount stores, supermarkets, yea even in record stores just like any less exceptional album.

It even is on various kinds of tape, those distributed by the slinky Ampex Corporation.

Pessimistic Note

It has not escaped Reprise's and Brother Records' attention that there will remain those yet unconvinced that an album called Surf's Up by The Beach Boys can come close to looking anything like today.

But you, doubting Tom, should remember that you once wore shorter hair, Pendletons, go-aheads and coveted monk's bumps.

And just as you've gone in another direction, so have they, to wit:

Once   Now

And so, haste not to judgment, because not only have The Beach Boys changed their heads, they also are more talented than you are.

Get this album, either the hard way or at your nearby record store.

You've done worse.

To: Surfin' Safari Time
Reprise Records
Burbank, Calif. 91505

Hi!
Enclosed in this box is my copy of the Beach Boys' Surfin' Safari album on Capitol, plus $1.00. Send me this best new Beach Boys album—The Beach Boys' Surf's Up—at no more cost to me. Thank you.

Name _____

Address _____

City _____ State _____ Zip _____

This offer valid only through 1971. Only one album to a customer, and we reserve the right to outlaw any thing sneaky we haven't anticipated. It'll take six weeks to get Surf's Up back to you, but the wait (if you can stand it) is well worthwhile. Offer is good only in the U.S.A.

159

Great Vibrations Week
July 4-10

David Brenner. July 1-5.
Friday through Tuesday, 8:30 & 11:30 PM. At Caesars Cabaret Theater. Tickets are $20 & $25, at Caesars Box Office, Ticketron, or Teletron.

Caesars Circus Maximus Circus. July 5, 6, 7, 9.
(Showtimes: Noon, 4PM, 8PM.) Tuesday, Wednesday, Thursday, and Saturday, under the bigtop. Missouri Avenue and the Boardwalk, next to Caesars. Tickets are $1.50 and $3.00, at the door. Produced by Bauer-Hall Enterprises.

World Championship PKA Knockout Karate. Friday, July 8, 7:30 PM.
See 3 World Championship bouts at Caesars Circus Maximus, at Missouri Avenue and the Boardwalk. Tickets are $10, $25, $50, at Caesars Box Office, Ticketron, or Teletron. You'll be pickin' up great vibrations as Caesars puts on a week-long July 4th entertainment

FREE Monday, July 4, 7:30 PM, The Beach Boys Concert.
On the beach in front of Caesars. Stay for the spectacular fireworks afterward.

The Pointer Sisters. July 6-10.
Wednesday through Sunday at Caesars Cabaret Theater, 8:30 & 11:30 PM. Tickets are $20 & $25, at Caesars Box Office, Ticketron, or Teletron.

WIN FREE CONCERT TICKETS

James Watt, our illustrious Secretary of the Interior, may not want the Beach Boys in Washington, D.C., but rock fans sure want them in Philly.

Those California dreamers will bring their beach-style rock 'n' roll to Philly's Mann Music Center on June 14. And the Sunday Times is giving away two free tickets to some lucky person to see the Beach Boys, live, at the Mann.

The Beach Boys have been around since the early 1960s. They're surfin' style has survived all the new, trendy waves in music and these guys are still going strong.

Some of their alltime hits include "California Girls," "Surfin' U.S.A.," "Help Me, Rhonda," "Little Deuce Coupe" and "I Get Around."

Don't miss out on this super chance to win free tickets to see these rock legends. To enter the Sunday Times Concert Contest, just fill out the entry and mail it to Box 270 in Springfield or drop it off at the Daily Times office in Primos.

You can enter as many times as you want — but no photocopies of the entry blank are acceptable. Everyone is eligible except Daily Times employees and their families.

The Sunday Times Concert Contest is run every week in the Sunday Times amusement section. The contest is held in conjunction with T. Morgan's rock music column which appears on page 14 in today's paper.

The lucky winner for the Beach Boys contest will be drawn at random on June 6. You could be the lucky person.

Even James Watt is invited to enter. If you'll remember, Mr. Watt banned the Beach Boys from a July 4 celebration on Washington's mall because the group "attracts the wrong element." Watt wanted someone more wholesome, like Wayne Newtown, to perform.

For all of you Bowie fans, we will be picking the winner for two tickets to the David Bowie contest tomorrow. The winner is notified by phone.

SURF'S UP Those never-say-retire Beach Boys are (front) Mike Love and Carl Wilson, (back) Brian Wilson, Al Jardine and Dennis Wilson. Those surfer boys will perform at the Mann Music Center on June 14.

Clip and Send

Beach Boys show

Name _____

Address _____

City & State _____

Zip _____

Phone _____

Mail to: **Concert Tickets**
P.O. Box 270
Springfield, Pa. 19064

161

162

LET'S GO to the
19 Canfield Fair 82
THE FAIR THAT MADE COUNTY FAIRS FAMOUS

"Something to Crow About"

FAIRGROUNDS REACHED:
VIA U.S. ROUTES 224, 62, OHIO 46, 14 AND OHIO TURNPIKE, I-76; I-80

GATE ADMISSION:
THURSDAY & FRIDAY $2.00
SATURDAY, SUNDAY & MONDAY $3.00

PARKING FREE PLUS SCORES OF FREE ATTRACTIONS!
RIDES BY INTERNATIONAL EXPOSITIONS, INC.

THURSDAY AND FRIDAY EVENINGS, SEPTEMBER 2nd and 3rd:
HARNESS RACING
POST TIME: 7:45 P.M.
BOXES: $2.00; RESERVED SEATS: $1.50
Afternoon Racing, Saturday and Monday. Post Time: 1:00 P.M.

SATURDAY EVENING, SEPTEMBER 4th:
THE BEACH BOYS
PERFORMANCES AT 7 AND 9 P.M.
SEATS RESERVED AT $8.00

SUNDAY MORNING, SEPTEMBER 5th — 11:30 A.M.
INVITATIONAL CHAMPIONSHIP TRUCK & TRACTOR PULL OFF
The climax of the June and July Elimination Pulls held at the Canfield Fairgrounds.
ALL SEATS $4.00

SUNDAY EVENING, SEPTEMBER 5th:
DONNY and MARIE OSMOND
and the OSMOND BROTHERS
25th ANNIVERSARY TOUR
PERFORMANCES AT 7 AND 9 P.M.
SEATS RESERVED AT $8.00

MONDAY EVENING, SEPTEMBER 6th:
PULL-O-RAMA
SUPER MODIFIED TRUCK PULL: TWO- AND FOUR-WHEEL-DRIVE TRUCKS IN A THREE-HOUR SPECTACULAR. PULL STARTS AT 6:00 P.M.
ALL SEATS AT $6.00

RAND LEVY—LOU FALCIGNO—
JIM PETERSON—JOHN GOURLEY
PRESENT

The Beach Boys

**FRIDAY
AUGUST 28—8 PM**

**BYRNE
MEADOWLANDS
ARENA**

Tickets on Sale Now

ALL SEATS RESERVED: $12.50 $10.50

TICKETS AVAILA... ...OFFICE & ALL USUAL
...PAYABLE TO M...
BOYS, MEADOWL... ...RUTHERFORD, NJ
07073. (...

...ATIN... ...DAY AT 3:00

In concert THE BEACH BOYS

**they've changed
even more than you**

SPECIAL ADDED SHOW SUN., SEPT. 2, 5 p.m.
TICKETS 3.85, 4.95, 6.05   MASSEY HALL
...Now on Sale: at Ticketron outlets, A & A Records downtown,
Music World Stores (Yorkdale, Fairview, Scarborough)

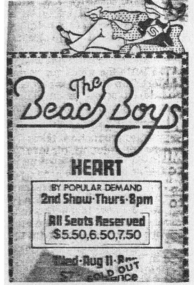

The Beach Boys

HEART

BY POPULAR DEMAND
2nd Show·Thurs·8pm

All Seats Reserved
$5.50, 6.50, 7.50

Wed·Aug 11·8...
S... ...ance

McCARTER THEATRE presents
The Beach Boys

DILLON GYMNASIUM of PRINCETON UNIVERSITY
FRIDAY, MAY 18 at 11 pm   8:00 pm SHOW SOLD OUT!

EXTRA ADDED PERF.

Tickets: $5.50, 5.00, 4.50 & 3.50. Now at McCarter Theatre box office, Princeton.
Also at all TICKETRON outlets (for locations: (212) 644-4400). Mail orders to McCarter
Theatre, Box 526, Princeton, N.J. 08540; please enclose stamped, self-addressed
envelope. PHONE ORDERS ACCEPTED (609) 921-8700.   ⊕TICKETRON

TUE·8pm

THE BEACH BOYS

$8.00 in advance
$9.00 day of show

JAMBORAMA

Jamboree Journal page 3

Beach Boys

Rock excites 75th Anniversary crowd

By STEVEN POCKRASS
Eagle Scout

As camera flashes danced in the dark night sky like northern lights, the true "boys of summer" proved at the 1985 National Scout Jamboree opening arena show that the Spirit indeed Lives On.

Although a little older, grayer and less in tune than they were in their prime, the boys who turned California beach music into an American institution had an audience of about 70,000 on their feet by the end of their show.

Scouts in the audience waited anxiously as Chief Scout Executive Ben Love made his introductions, hoping each time that it would be time for the feature band.

They, the Beach Boys, appeared on stage clad in beach clothes and Jamboree neckerchiefs. Two large screens made the show visible to everyone in the arena. As lights shone and cameras clicked, the musicians opened with "California Girls," a tune recently revived by Van Halen star David Lee Roth.

Beach balls were bounced around the arena as the band played three more songs. After that introductory set, lead vocalist Mike Love told the audience, "We've never played anything this unique."

The crowd answered with a roar, and the crooners sang a recent release, "Getcha Back." Three songs later, the band played a loud, lively version of "I Get Around," "We Could Be Happy" and "It's Getting Late," with the latter two featuring Brian Wilson solos.

It was not until the final two songs, however, that the somewhat reserved crowd was brought to its feet with "Surfin' Safari" and "Surfin' U.S.A." Scouts dancing, "surfing" on the arena grass and chanting for "one more song."

After having already performed fifteen tunes, the Beach Boys came back on stage and responded with four more songs to the crowd's delight.

"I was a Boy Scout once too, you know," Al Jardine told the standing spectators.

"California Calling," was followed by "Good Vibrations," one of the most rousing songs of the show. Scouts tossed patches to the band, and at least one threw his shirt on-stage.

Flags waved, Scouts sang and yelled "Yeah" with the pros, who closed out the show with "Barbara Ann" and, most appropriately, "Fun, Fun, Fun."

But while the Beach Boys were indeed the feature band, many other groups kept the spirit alive with song and dance.

Then the 130-member National Scout Jamboree Band played a selection of marches and other songs. "I don't think it's a hit yet," said Dean Hunkapiller, as he waited to go onstage. Hunkapiller plays the alto saxophone.

They were followed by the Israeli Scout Friendship Caravan, a coed group which performs at camps and communities around the eastern portion of the United States. The young men and women sang and danced to a variety of Hebrew and American songs.

Next came the Good Time Country Show from Busch Gardens at Williamsburg, Va.

"I think it's going to be fun," said featured singer Beth-Marie McGeney before the show. McGeney said the group members auditioned independently for Busch Gardens and have been playing contemporary country selections as a band since the summer began.

The crown size was a big change for the 4-woman, 3-man band, which McGeney said plays before an average audience of about 500 at each Busch Gardens show.

After the Beach Boys was a production on the history of Scouting. The closing act before the weary crowd was the Great American Entertainment Company, a group of 56 college performers who entertained President Reagan at the 1985 Presidential inaugural. They performed a 20-minute "Salute to America."

DRAMA JAMBORAMA

with ...

Philip E. Davis

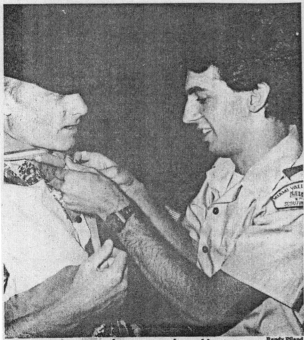

...And much goodwill...

Randy Piland

...Harmony and guitars.

Philip E. Da

Beach Boy Season

WITH THE 41ST International Eucharistic Congress opening the month and the Federation Cup Tennis closing it out August is a very busy and prestige-laden month for The Spectrum. These two events combine with the slower pace of our summer schedule to briefly eclipse the usually heavy music scene. But, fear not stout-hearted music freaks, September holds all sorts of goodies soon-to-be-announced. Until then, we'll try to keep your adrenaline level reasonably high with the **Beach Boys** on Aug. 11 and 12 (Wed. and Thurs.) and the **AVERAGE WHITE BAND** on Aug. 17 (Tues.).

This current national tour of the **BEACH BOYS** is taking place amid difficult and confusing circumstances. For the first time since his nervous breakdown in 1964, **Brian Wilson** is touring with the group and also has produced their first studio album in four years, "15 Big Ones" (released last month). So far, the album has been greeted with less than hosannas by the critics, but since it's been so long-awaited by the faithful, it's selling better than A.T.&T.

* * *

UNFORTUNATELY, Wilson's re-emergence poses certain internal problems for the group as a whole. As one of the group's three founding Wilson brothers, he was their composer, producer, and the creator of the BEACH BOYs' distinctive sound, a unique use of choral harmony which was even copied and assimilated by the **BEATLES**. As a result of Brian's withdrawal in '64, the other members of the group were forced to develop their own creative resources; which they did most successfully. Each member evolved into a composer in his own right, and Brian's younger brother **Carl** very successfully took over as the group's record producer.

Now that their original guiding spirit has re-asserted himself, it's going to be interesting watching the BEACH BOYS' future unravel. Considering that they've become fully developed performers with the ego expectations of adults, it's hard to imagine the group being willing or able to relinquish control of their musical and professional direction to Brian for long. Or as that old song said, you can't keep them down on the farm after they've seen Par-e-e-e.

* * *

Action Rock Stars o

AL JARDINE   MIKE LOVE   CARL WILSON   ROCKY FATAAR   DENNIS WILSON

'76 Version

Appearing

At Spectrum

Aug. 11-12

ACTION CAT will be there, for sure.

DENNIS WILSON

the Planet

MAY 16 — MAY 23, 1979

THE BEACH BOYS' CARL WILSON

MICHAEL J. FERGUSON

MUSIC

The Beach Boys Surf On

If there is one red-blooded, all-American band that qualifies as an institution, it has to be those bronzed poets of California sun 'n' surf, the Beach Boys. Known the world over for their bright, breezy odes to perennial pleasure, this venerable group and their music have spanned two decades and delivered a body of sounds that literally created a "California Mystique," as their most famous songs celebrated the adolescent search for high-spirited good times. Most of all, the Beach Boys, whose creative spirit is propelled by the talents of the brothers Wilson, have endured and continued to grow, as their most recent recording "L.A. (Light Album)" certainly attests.

Beginning their career in the early Sixties as Kenny and the Cadets, the Beach Boys skyrocketed to national attention with their single "Surfin'" became a regional hit and garnered a contract with Capitol Records. Based on simple three-cord, Chuck Berry-styled progressions, their early songs were immensely listenable snapshots that sang the praises of life under the always-shining California Sun, a lifestyle eventually imitated (or at least fantasized about) by teenagers everywhere. The message and philosophy were strikingly direct: all that mattered was the next thrill, and Nirvana was discovered upon encountering the "Perfect Wave."

With Brian Wilson at the helm, brothers Carl and Dennis, cousin Mike Love and friend Al Jardine plotted a course that was to define and articulate much of the essence of the youth-oriented culture of the early Sixties and included an incredible string of hit records. Combining pure, shimmering harmonies (learned from early Four Freshmen and Everly Brothers styles) and ethereal musical landscapes, the Beach Boys brought a child-like innocence and clarity of vision to popular music that has long been copied, but rarely convincingly duplicated.

Their early songs were sincere, open, honest expressions of the world they saw around them, a world of fast cars, cute girls, pounding surf and crusin' for burgers. "Surfer Girl," "Catch A Wave," "Little Deuce Coupe," "In My Room," "Fun Fun Fun" and countless others provided the soundtrack. Within these cheerful, optimistic performances (even when they lost at love the Beach Boys sounded like a choir), every element of the quixotic American Dream was revealed.

When the mid-Sixties brought about a shifting of emphasis to various political and social concerns, the group fell into a temporary period of disfavor among the pseudo-hip elite, who regarded them as practioners of bubble-gum. This was unfortunate, as some of the band's best, most adventurous music was produced in this era. Of particular note was the loose, informal, live "Beach Boys Party" and the ground-breaking, densley orchestral "Pet Sounds," an ambitious experiment that broke many barriers and compared favorably with producer Phil Spector's best work. Ignored and /or rejected by the record-buying public, the inability of "Pet Sounds" to make an impression was the beginning of Brian's reclusive period, even though the record was eventually hailed as a classic.

As the Beatles, Stones and others moved into areas of personal exploration, so did the Beach Boys. This most effected Brian who reportedly retreated into a kind of netherworld where he was rumored to spend long hours writing songs in a sandbox constructed in his living room. His eccentricities aside, Brian was obsessed with the creation of a symphonic rock masterwork, the legendary "Smile." It was never to be, however, as the tapes were lost in a studio fire which Brian took as an omen, disbanding the album ("Smiley Smile," containing scraps of the original, was finally released to critical applause and public bewilderment, nonetheless

yielding to two conceptually advanced hits, "Good Vibrations" and "Heroes and Villans"). Although the group was no longer enormously popular, Brian was gaining a reputation as a compositional genius, a fact which the infant rock press rhapsodized to quasi-intellectual extremes.

As the Sixties wore on, the Beach Boys reached a commercial impasse, continuing to release exceptional records which were critical favorites, but commercial bombs. With Brian in the shadows, Bruce Johnston was brought into the group and immediately his presence was felt. At the close of the decade, the group releaed a trio of spiritually-linked, slightly funky, pleasant, unpretentious records that solidified their creative force, if not their cumulative earnings. "Wild Honey," "Friends" and "20 /20," lightly regarded at the time of their release, are now recognized as minor classics essential to the band's evolution.

In the early Seventies, the band experienced a renaissance of sorts. With Brian returning to a more productive role and the others developing their talents, they released a series of polished, progressive pop LPs which enjoyed increased sales and renewed airplay. Another curious event occurred: the group stirred live audiences again. With their older audience receiving the most enthusiastic response, they rekindled the interest of old fans and gained a new generations of listeners who were just discovering them.

Then, a two-record set of greatest hits called "Endless Summer" was unleashed to unprecedented reaction, as the album became a huge seller and established the Beach Boys once again as a top concert draw. Of course, it put the group in a quandry, as they continued to offer new material to an audience thirsting mostly for nostalgia.

Recent years have seen more personnel shake-ups, and leadership

emphasis within the band has shifted several times. Bruce Johnston left, replaced by Blondie Chaplin and Ricky Faatar, who gave them a funkier flavor. At the same time, it seemed as though Carl might assume leadership. This didn't happen, however, as Brian made a comeback, producing "Love You" and "Fifteen Big Ones," which contain moments of pristine, luxuriant technique.

Reaching a nadir of sorts with their last release for Reprise, the Beach Boys have recovered with a promising venture for Columbia, the newly-released, briskly-selling "L.A.," which features (gulp!) a ten-minute DISCO-ized reworking of "Here Comes The Night." But before you swallow your surfboard, it should be noted that the song (from "Wild Honey") was rhythm-and- blues based and besides, there's the suspicion here that the boys had tongues planted firmly in cheek when devising this rendition. Also of importance is the return of Bruce Johnston in the role of producer and the indication that he'll return to the group.

For almost twenty years, the Beach Boys have provided us with a sunny backdrop. Despite occasional lapses, the mythology they created persists as perhaps one of the more valid views of the American Way of Life. If they have seemed irrelevant at times, one need only remember their amazing resiliency, their instinctive ability to brush failure aside and recapture their collective muse. Always a family, they have weathered inner turmoil and remained faithful to their vision. In the process, the Beach Boys have developed a highly personal, unmistakably distinct style that is known and loved everywhere. And the chances are quite good that when they return to the Spectrum next week, they'll play one of your all-time favorite songs. May they catch that wave forever!

The Beach Boys will appear at the Spectrum May 21.

The Best One Yet

The Old/New Beach Boys Really Come Down Hard!

By DON MENEFEE

As everyone knows, there are concerts and then, there are CONCERTS! Let-me-tell-you, this past Friday, I went to a CONCERT!

After a bit of schedule changing involving Spooky Tooth, Frampton's Camel and Rory 'someone-or-another', the Spectrum's lights went up on one of the finest musical events ever offered by Larry Magid et al (otherwise known as the Electric Factory).

It's blatant statement time: The Beach Boys are possibly the finest rock 'n roll band in the world! How's that Blues freaks? But, more of that later.

The concert got under way on time for once with a very little-known group who shall always remain that way, Rory 'what's his name'.

Musically, very tight, Rory absolutely blew it with the amount of volume they put out. Yes fans, you're hearing it. They were way too loud. I saw many people cover their ears and run for the exits.

I never thought I'd say a concert was too loud. But there it is.

THE SECOND portion of this three-part event was a little better, but not all that great. I realize I may be putting my life on the line. But, Argent just ain't that good.

Aside from their now famous "Hold Your Head Up," Argent didn't exactly put the crowd on their ears. Matter-of-fact, you might say people were starting to get bored.

I think one thing that sort of rubbed me the wrong way was the way they left the stage.

I'm a firm believer in leaving as 'Champ'. In other words, leave the fans with a good taste in their faces by doing your absolute best material and

leave the stage. If you're going to have an encore, save the best for last and go out on top.

We're all bright enough to know, every group plans at least one encore. Personally, I think they'd come back even if no one wanted them.

Anyway, Argent did "Hold Your Head Up" and got the crowd as high as a kite. Screaming "Thank you, we love you!" they left the stage as kings of the concert and then made the mistake.

Being high, the fans ranted and raved for "more, more, more!" and Argent gave it to them. What a shame.

When they came back out, they made some feeble attempt at some '50's stuff and blew it. They couldn't have gotten an encore if their lives depended on it. In this case, it's last impressions which are the most important.

ON TO THE goodies... While up in the press box, waiting for the appearance of the Beach boys, some young chap ran up to me in the dark, handed me a box and blasted out the door, almost in a panic. I didn't really see him, but the box he gave me did hold a great deal of interest. It was almost chock full of fresh, red strawberries. And I'm a strawberry freak!

Ed Weiner, public relations mogul at the Spectrum, asked me "Why did Dennis Wilson give you those things?" How about that! I had some honest-to-goodness Beach Boys strawberries! And they were delicious! I was off to a good start.

After assorted equipment

On the Rascals' last night in Hawaii, Tom Moffatt had a sv luau for them. Surprise guest was Beach Boy Dennis Wilson

problems (which didn't m much) 20,000 people w absolutely jolted to their fee "Surfin' USA" done as we remember it. Only the st The 'Boys' interspersed s of their brand new musi with the old and much to surprise, it was very, good. Some of the mate from their newest offer simply called, "Holland," really good music.

This, plus the addition Blondie Chaplain, a nativ South Africa, has added a dimension to their music. old Beach boys are still tl and still fantastic. But, sure have grown up.

I HAVE NEVER seen, in 75-plus concert experier excitement absolutely pou from an audience. The p box was a mess. Usuall pretty business-like place was jumpin' with pe flinging themselves about all matter of the dance.

The most amazing thing the crowd. Though billed : dance concert, I've never : anyone dance on the giant rink floor. Friday was tot different. Do you have any of what 11,000 people look when they dance?

The Beach Boys played danced their way through likes of (listen to th California Girls; Sloop Johr Good Vibrations; Help Rhonda; Fun Fun Fun; Su Girl and Good Vibrations. all that new stuff I mentic before.

At one point they had all frantic 20,000 singing in mony! Really delightful.

About midnight the 'B left the stage for their atte at an encore. Nobody got up we knew they'd be back. If

(Please Turn To Next Page

THE PITTSBURGH
Phonograph
Record Magazine

5th Annual

Norman Seeff's Rock Star Exhibition

Dennis Wilson

Mike Love

Carl Wilson

Al Jardine

BEACH BOYS!

September, 1977

Free From WDVE

"We're still happening. New people are picking up on us all the time. I don't really analyze why we're successful, but the main reason for our popularity has to be the songs themselves." --Brian Wilson

By HARVEY KUBERNIK

If anyone can judge the physical and creative renaissance of Brian Wilson, it's Earle Mankey, the house engineer at Brother Studio in Santa Monica.

I've attended a few Wilson/Mankey sessions in the last few months and their afternoon playbacks are a lot better than most of the gigs I've seen all year.

Mankey is an unassuming character, formerly a member of Sparks. Along with Kim Fowley he's co-produced the Runaways, Helen Reddy and the Quick albums, as well as engineering some of Elton John's "Blue Moves" and the new Eric Carmen album.

We're listening to a rough mix of the new American Spring single, tentatively titled "Heaven." It's an ambitious track of irresistible pop/rock to which Brian wants to add a few more instruments.

Earle remembers the first time he did a session with Brian. "About a year and a half ago, before '15 Big Ones' was released, we did some basic tracks, and Brian was very tense in the studio. We recorded a version of 'Ding Dang', and a few weeks later waxed a song called 'Back Home.'

"Things started clicking, Earle recalls. "Carl came into the booth when we were playing back the track and said, 'Earle! This is the way it used to be! This is it! You're seeing it! It's happening now!"

"Brian took his time to get re-acquainted with the studio. I've seen how the papers and media used to portray him as a hopeless child. Brian is Brian. He's funny, witty and very honest. Musically each subsequent album we do gets better and better. The last album, 'Beach Boys Love You,' Brian came in and did it instead of being forced into it."

Mankey also remembers the day Brian said he was going to tour with the Beach Boys. "He plugged in his bass and practised to a Ronettes album. I was blown out when I saw him on stage at the Forum. I never thought he would tour with the Beach Boys again. Things are cooking in the studio, based on the positive things that went down on the last tour.

"Brian seems more secure in his position. He's running smoothly. The biggest difference between '15 Big Ones' and 'Beach Boys Love You' is that Brian played most of the tracks himself. Eighty per cent of the instruments. It's very easy to work with Brian. There's a lot of speed in what he does.

"The new songs for the next album are more developed. The thing about the Beach Boys that people never understand is that their music has always been simplistic, even though the productions may not seem that way."

Mankey then spins the next Beach Boys album, slated for a September issue, which might be called "Adult Child". "Life Is For The Living," "Hey There Little Tom Boy," "Deep Purple," "Help Is On The Way," "It's Over Now," "Everyone's Got To Live," "Shortnin' Bread," "Lines," "On Broadway," "Games," "Base Ball" and "Still I Dream Of It." Some of the tunes are two years old and originally intended for "15 Big Ones."

Also in the can is a frantic reworking of the old Spencer Davis hit, "Gimme Some Lovin'." "Brian wants to work," says Earle. "He's looking for a goal. Some of the new songs reflect his everyday situation, like 'Help Is On The Way.'

"It's getting easier to write songs," explains Brian.

Wilson lost 50 pounds since the last time I saw him, and looks healthy. He spits his words out quickly. We talk about his songwriting.

"I don't carry a notebook or use a tape player," he begins. "I like to tell a story in the songs with as few words as possible. I sort of tend to write what I've been through and look inside myself. Some of the songs are messages."

Yet Brian's lyrics have never been cosmic wordplays. "I've always been insecure about my lyrics. I always felt that what I wanted to say was never really imparted in my lyrics—that the message just wasn't there.

"I'm extremely confident that the group will always get some worthwhile message across in some way. With the new album **The Beach Boys Love You** there are a lot of simple you-me type lyrics, like the Beatles did in their early songs."

"The changes in Brian have been very visible, very heartening and satisfying to observe".

Rodney Bingenheimer arrives on the scene. Brian hugs the lad. "Rodney is as cool as honey," he grins. Bingenheimer now has a top-rated radio programme on KROQ-AM, and recently did a two-hour salute to Brian on his 35th birthday.

Through glitter or this latest punk period, Bingenheimer has always played Beach Boys records. "I first met Brian and the Beach Boys at a concert in San Jose in 1963," he says.

"One time I went to a Phil Spector recording session when he was doing 'River Deep, Mountain High'. Brian, Mick Jagger and myself were all in the room next to Phil. When Phil records, it's a performance, an act. When Brian records it's a very serious thing.

"Every week on my programme kids call from all over L.A. and ask if I can play some Beach Boys records. After I play 'Surfer Girl' or 'Mona' from the new album, more people will ring and ask where they can buy the record or who was that playing. The Beach Boys have outlasted all the fads."

Rodney and I have an argument regarding the new Ramone's single, "Sheena Is A Punk Rocker." I say it's pinched from the Sun Rays' "I Live For The Sun" and "Little Honda," a tune Brian penned for the Hondells. Rod says goodbye to all in attendance and proclaims, "the Beach Boys have always had the best-looking girls at their concerts." And winking, he adds, "the Beach Boys are permanent wave!"

Earle, Brian and myself then reminisce about Phil Spector. "The man is my hero," Brian enthuses. "He gave rock 'n' roll just what it needed at the time and obviously influenced us a lot. His productions...they're so large and emotional. Powerful... the Christmas album is still one of my favourites."

I remember checking out Brian's record collection. McCartney, Stevie Wonder and Fleetwood Mac were current tops, but his old Ronettes and Crystals 45s were so worn-out from constant play that the grooves became mirror-like.

"It's kinda funny," says Brian. "The Bay City Rollers did one of our songs, and now B.J. Thomas has a hit with 'Don't Worry Baby.' Shaun Cassidy has a number one record with Phil's 'Da Doo Ron Ron,' and this group Kiss has just done 'Then She Kissed Me.'

"We've done a lot of Phil's songs: 'I Can Hear Music,' 'Just Once In My Life,' 'There's No Other,' 'Chapel Of Love'...I used

Brian & Marylin Wilson—July, 1977.

to go to his sessions and watch him record. I learned a lot..."

"I've always been flattered that Brian continues to say nice things about me and keeps recording my songs," said Fairfax High School graduate and man-in-the-mansion Phil Spector. "Brian is a very sweet guy and a nice human being. I'm glad he's coming out of his shell. I think he got caught in a trap with 'Good Vibrations.' I think he got condemned more than condoned.

"He became a prisoner instead of a poet. He had the plaudits, the accolades and touched the masses. I know music is a very important thing to him, besides a vocation. It became cluttered the last few years. Your attitude is in the grooves, and it's a very personal thing. But Brian thrived on competition.

"I remember when 'Fun Fun Fun' came out. He wasn't interested in the money, but a top ten record. He wanted to know how the song would do against the Beatles and if KFWB would play it. But I never saw Brian as a competitor."

The next day I travel to American Productions, where the Beach Boys minus Mike Love are rehearsing at noon. Everyone is present. Besides Al Jardine, Carl, Dennis and Brian Wilson, there are also the auxiliary musicians who take the studio sound to the stage.

Carly Munoz, Billy Hinsche and Elmo Peter are the keyboardists, Eddy Carter plays bass, Bobby Figuera supplies percussion, and the horn players are Lance Buller, John Foss, Michael Andreas, Rod Novak and Charlie McCarthy Jr.

Their live show is approximately two hours and 45 minutes long, the songs the group has been performing the last five years.

"A lot of the kids coming to see us now weren't even born when the first surfing hits were recorded in 1961. For a long time we refused to sing stuff like 'Surfin' U.S.A.'." Carl once mentioned in an interview. "But finally we realized that we were resisting our own history. Now we've learned to embrace our past."

During a break in the action, Elmo Peter, who has been with the Beach Boys since October, 1975, talks about his two-year stint with the definitive American group.

Elmo comes from a classical background and confessed that as a youth he really wasn't knocked out by the Beach Boys or the Four Seasons. "The high harmonies used to turn me off. But I love playing with the Beach Boys now.

"It's pretty similar to playing with an orchestra. Parts are mapped out and things are pretty specific and refined."

I tell him that I'm really pleased to see Brian back at the piano and leading the rehearsal. "The changes in Brian have been very visible since I joined the touring line-up," he says.

"Very heartening and satisfying to observe. Brian's really takin' care of business." He also reveals that the Beach Boys are scheduled for a trip to Japan, Australia and New Zealand at the end of the year.

Later in the afternoon Brian and myself retire to a small office away from the music and noise.

"I'm looking forward to touring. Artists like Paul McCartney, Elton John have always said nice things about the Beach Boys and myself. We've influenced a lot of groups, especially our harmonies: Electric Light Orchestra, 10cc, Queen."

What about the Beach Boys' longevity?

"We're still happening. New people are picking up on us all the time. I don't really analyze why we're successful. I'm sure the Beach Boys are viewed as an institution, but the main reason for our popularity has to be the songs.

"I didn't ever think I would be back touring with the Beach Boys again. They asked me to do it and I said OK. It's like racketball (Brian's favourite sport along with basketball). You make a commitment once you get on the court. The other guy serves and you have to play."

Wilson's official return to the stage was July 1976 at Oakland Stadium, California. Early shows were full of chaos, bodyguards, and general hoopla.

"I feel more into it now. Rehearsals went real good. I got some of the old fire back, and I feel more positive. I feel good about myself, and once you feel good about yourself and accept yourself, you can touch other people. I lost weight and acquired self-discipline.

DENNIS WILSON

By MITCH COHEN

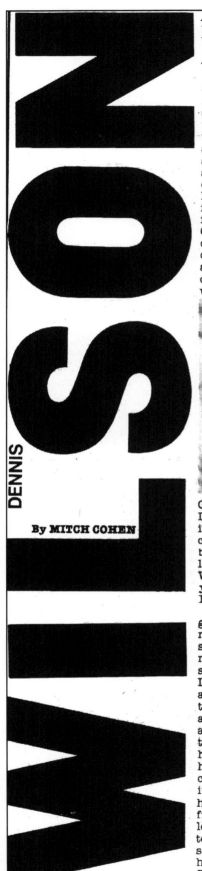

Dennis Alone: "A turbulent combination of the rough and the polished."

"We do solo projects for ourselves," Dennis Wilson said during an interview eighteen months ago. "There are hundreds of tunes that we've recorded, a tremendous amount of solo things. We're in our studio every day, but we don't put it out. It's a hobby." He also emphatically denied any group or individual move to Jim Guercio's Caribou Records, saying that they owed Reprise three more albums. A few weeks after our conversation, there was a press release from CBS Records stating that Dennis would be embarking on a part time solo career, on Caribou. The band signed with the label less than a year later. Which goes to show that you can't always believe a Beach Boy.

Considering that other group members have been more prolific, and have stepped out front vocally more often, it may take some by surprise that Dennis is the first to break away, to take two LP sides, twelve songs, for himself away from the Beach Boys, as cohesive and self-contained a unit as rock music has seen. After all, Dennis has rarely seemed the pop careerist: liner notes have it that he fell asleep when he was supposed to cut his first studio lead vocal; he left to make a movie; he temperamentally kept his songs off **Surf's Up**. Until his four contributions to **Sunflower**, he was hardly considered a songwriting contender, especially with big brother Brian around.

But on his Caribou debut, **Pacific Ocean Blue**, the youngest Wilson brother, the unpredictable Beach Boy, the one who got the whole thing rolling by suggesting that Brian write a song about surfboarding, has made an LP that can stand on its own merits as a work of individuality, brooding romanticism and musical integrity. This is no beach party, and although some of the modes and concepts are familiar, Brian being Dennis' most conspicuous influence as a composer—particularly in the overlaying and juxtaposition of instruments for textural effect—this album very rarely sounds like Beach Boys outtakes. Dennis has found his own path to the ocean, and the result probably coincides only tangentially with your idea of what a Dennis Wilson album might be.

The first things to get past on the way towards an appreciation of the album are the departures: the raw, abrasive edge of Dennis' voice; the lack of sprightliness in the melodies; the untraditional song structures. Much of the album is a turbulent combination of the rough and the polished, as simple lyrics collide with demanding arrangements, raspy vocals compete with impeccably produced musical tracks. It's a record of extremes, a moody, personal California album complete with failed ambition and audacious successes.

"River Song," co-written with Carl Wilson, eases you in to **Pacific Ocean Blue** with recognizable elements, multiple voices, dense overdubbing, a lyrical paean to water, Dennis slam-dunk drumming. It's a wonderful track filled with Beach Boy dynamics, and it introduces one of the album's dominant themes, the lure, the omnipresence and the abuse of nature. Events and emotions in Dennis' songs are often compared to natural phenomena, and many have sounds of nature as a backdrop. One song is called "Moonshine," another "Rainbows." "Love comes and goes like sunshine" on the graceful "Thought of You," and on "Dreamer," we're asked to let the wind carry our blues away. Love gone bad is as dust to water. The album's title song, "Pacific Ocean Blues," written with Mike Love (all the LP's songs but one, a solo composition, are Dennis Wilson collaborations, most frequently with Greg Jakobson), is an indictment of the slaughter of seals and whales, and the oceanic Pet Sound/effects on the following track make "Farewell My Friend" sound like a paired eulogy to the murdered mammals.

The other major motif on the LP is theatrical, life seen as an imitation of art. There are a number of references to the playing of music—as on "What's Wrong" the album's obligatory rock and roll anthem—and to Dennis as a musician. "Moonshine" has a line about the breaking off of a relationship being like the end of a play, and the final track, "End of the Show," picks up the metaphor of the link between the staged and the real. At the close of the album it all comes

continued from previous page

together, love, nature and theatre. It can't be just my imagination that the applause and whistles that come at the "End of the Show" can be mistaken for the sounds of waves and chirping birds.

All this thematic extrapolation aside, the best part of **Pacific Ocean Blue** is the way that Dennis Wilson weaves together contradictory ideas; the way that repetition of a horn pattern on "Time" can sound both chaotic and controlled; the way that the short, ominous "Friday Night" gets across musically the appeal and the dangers of cutting loose for a weekend; the way abrupt changes in tone and sudden bursts of instruments both disrupt and complete musical thoughts.

At times Wilson goes overboard with clutter, taking his brother's **Pet Sounds** aural sophistication and experimentation a little too far, and misses the vocal equipment necessary to bring the level of the singing up to the adventurousness of the tracks (both B. Wilson and P. Spector knew that grandiose concepts demand great voices). But when he pulls it off, **Pacific Ocean Blue** is a unique, offbeat Los Angeles tapestry by a man who's always been more complex than he's seemed. Like his brother, Dennis shows real talent as a minimalist, using brief blocks of musical time to their fullest, compressing a lot of information into a limited space, constantly shifting the sand under our feet. And like almost everything any of the Beach Boys has been involved in this decade (excepting interim BB Bruce Johnston's sluggard **Going Public**), his album defies initial expectations, takes a while to come into its own. But it does, and gives Carl, Al and Mike something to live up to when the time comes for them to solo.

Join The Beach Boys and their special guest stars Glen Campbell, Belinda Carlisle, Ray Charles, Patrick Duffy, The Everly Brothers, Jeffrey Osborne and many more to celebrate 25 years of Beach Boy music and "Good Vibrations."

The Beach Boys
25 YEARS TOGETHER

AN ABC SPECIAL
8:30 PM abc 6 7

BRIAN WILSON
genius or madman?

by Jim Girard

Brian has created the finest music of his time...

Andy Kent

Brian Wilson has been called many things — from "genius" (a common handle) to "madman" (an equally severe description). As the driving force behind America's well-respected Beach Boys, Brian Wilson has created the finest music of his time. He is both the most overrated and most underrated talent in the music profession. Is he crazy? I don't know. After speaking with him I still don't know. Although his mental condition has been the (labored) topic of one too many features in the rock press, he shows no outward signs of being lost forever. He is neurotic (by his own admission) and shy, but he communicates just fine in his music. Come to think of it, for all of his supposed mental problems, Brian Wilson is more mild-mannered and cordial than 90 percent of his peers.

Brian answers questions in short, but direct answers. Often, sometimes to the point of distraction, Brian will answer a seemingly easy question with a plain "I don't know." He doesn't lie, anyway.

What Brian has to say is said in his music. All of the recent rock press — all of the cover stories and strenuously-pressed reports about his wanton ways — has proven that trying to figure out a man like Brian Wilson or trying to dissect him like some freak in a circus is totally useless. They were spinning their wheels. Not only that, their cruelty (hidden behind some masked journalistic crusade) was unforgivable.

With *15 Big Ones*, Brian took the entire country on a nostalgic trip, bringing us an album of half oldies and half original material. With *The Beach Boys Love You*, however, Brian Wilson has compiled a totally original batch of songs; no oldies for filler, this time.

It looks as if Brian Wilson is totally back in the saddle. To stress the point, Brian even notified his publicists to line up some interviews to talk about the new album and just to say hello to a few people. Little did I think that Brian would call *exactly* on time for his HIT PARADER interview though. He did.

I mentioned that I knew he was moving and wondered if he'd built a studio in his new home. "No," said Brian. "I still live in BelAir here and I'm calling from home now. I was thinking of getting another home, but we have decided to stay here. We've lived here for eight years."

By "we" Brian means he and his wife, Marilyn Wilson.

Brian was chipper and alert during our interview, but didn't offer too many

He is both the most overrated and underrated talent in the music profession.

I asked Brian if he read all of the stories people have been writing about him.

"I don't like to read about me as much as I used to, but I still do. I do like to read about The Beach Boys. Criticism doesn't offend me; I just take it. It never got me too upset, no." says Brian.

"Hey, have you heard Dennis' album?" he asks.

I told him that I had talked to Dennis a few months back and he told me all about *Pacific Ocean Blue*, his first solo album. Brian seemed satisfied.

Most of all, Brian Wilson was enthusiastic about *Beach Boys Love You*. Brian said: *"The Beach Boys Love You* was much harder to finish than the last one (*15 Big Ones*). It was much harder for us because it was all new songs, you know. It took a longer time to make. Real hard."

Songs from *15 Big Ones*, Brian explained, were either oldies, of course, or original songs that weren't really new — ones that had been laying around on tape for years. Only a handful of tracks were written specifically for that album. Hence, the looseness of the package. Brian explains: "Like 'Back Home' is really old. It was originally written in 1962, but it never got finished. 'Back Home' was recorded, but never used. Other things were like that."

On *Beach Boys Love You*, all the songs are originals. All were written within the past year or so and Brian plays a larger role in the creation of this album than he has in a Beach Boys album since *Pet Sounds* in 1966.

"Of the fourteen songs on the album, I sing six — can't remember which ones though. I think my favorite songs on the album are 'Airplane' and 'The Night Was So Young'," Brian says.

I asked Brian if The Beach Boys really had *another* whole album finished. "Yes," he said. "We recorded two albums at the same time, sort of. The other one is finished, but we don't have a title yet and the tracks aren't mixed or anything. I have no idea when it would come out either."

Needless to say, Brian has been involved in quite a lot of recording as of late. Not only were two Beach Boys albums being recorded at Brother Studios (their own studio in Santa Monica, CA), but also a Dennis Wilson solo album, plus Eric Carmen was doing vocals for his second album there as well. With everything buzzing, Brian found himself working overtime. Dennis would even work a split shift, so to speak; he'd do sessions with the band from 9 am until 2 pm each day and cut tracks for his solo lp during the evening hours.

(Eric Carmen was amazed to discover he could barely book time there to do a few vocal sessions. Ex-Beach Boy Bruce Johnston was working with Carmen on his vocal backgrounds, when they discovered that they needed another part — one that Carl Wilson could sing perfectly. "When I called Carl," Eric Carmen explains, "he told me he would love to sing the part on the song, but it was his anniversary. He told me to call Brian. I did and Brian came down; he sang the part." The song is called "She Did It" — check it out.)

Dennis said, "It's really a treat to have all five of us back on the road playing together. With Brian back it isn't a chore anymore."

It's the way it always should have been.

true. I couldn't elaborate on that though, but I feel that it is definitely true."

As I hung up the phone with Brian, I thought of something Dennis had told me some months back about just how important it is to all of The Beach Boys to have Brian back. He said: "It's really been a treat with the five of us back on the road and playing together. Really good. Brian just decided he wanted to do it again, you know. With Brian back it isn't a chore anymore. We love him; now it's the way it should have been."

Considering that *The Beach Boys Love You* is such a vibrant tribute to American life — complete with Brian's paean to "Johnny Carson" — I would tend to agree with Dennis' statement. Now, it *is* the way it should have always been. □

When I mentioned Eric Carmen to Brian, he said that he loved Eric Carmen. Did he notice a strong influence that Carmen had gotten from him? "In some ways I can see where I have influenced him to a point, but I can't really tell just how or where," Brian says modestly.

I knew I had to ask Brian about his Saturday Night Live performance some months back. Of course, everyone knows he was nervous and sweaty, but did he regret playing solo on national TV?

"Oh, no," Brian says. "They just hired some musicians to play in the background and I did 'Back Home' and 'Love Is A Woman' from the new album. I did 'Good Vibrations' too. My doctor at the time thought I should do it, so I did it. I enjoyed it. Yes, very much. The others, my brothers that is, they liked it a lot too."

I knew that it wasn't good to get too philosophical with Brian Wilson, especially on the telephone. I did want to get his reaction to something Van Dyke Parks (who co-wrote several songs with Brian years ago) said about music being Brian's best friend — the thing that never betrayed him. Did he agree with that? Brian answered a polite "Yes." He softly said: "Music *is* my best friend. I feel that is

"Music is my best friend," Brian agreed. "I feel that is true."

Stuart G. Ihen

Andy Kent

181

Aaron/Morley

SURFS UP FOR THE BEACH BOYS

by Jim Girard

Like all established supergroups, The Beach Boys have their share of problems. For the past 17 years, they have been, more or less, the unabashed kings of surf music. They have evolved and changed with the times and have always managed to remain in tune with their roots. Even more than The Rolling Stones, The Beach Boys are the grandfathers of rock. All of the members of the group are well into their 30's and have their own interests.

The stability of the group unit has sometimes been shaky. However, The Beach Boys have always remained on the road — even when they weren't having hit records or making them at all. Therefore, The Beach Boys have always played to younger and younger crowds all of the time. At your average Beach Boys show today, the age range is from 12 to 40. That's scary, isn't it?

One reason that people will always love The Beach Boys is because as people they are real. Brothers Carl, Dennis

and, of course, Brian Wilson are all very different personalities. Alan Jardine and Mike Love have always been at the helm of the group though; the bulk of the lead singing is done by Mike Love.

Recently, Mike Love was playing a concert with his band, Celebration, and we were doing an interview and discussing the vulnerability of The Beach Boys. And although Mike Love is involved with fellow meditators with Celebration, and also with his own solo recording project, he remains totally concerned with the future of The Beach Boys.

Last year, it seems, The Beach Boys almost broke up. A public fight (backstage at an outdoor show) and a lot of bad - rapping followed by various members. Being basically a family band, The Beach Boys did weather that particular storm. Mike Love

reports all is well. He flipped on a cassette of the new studio album, *Winds Of Change*, as proof.

What flowed from the speakers of my JVC player was not an incomplete bunch of ditties like their last album, *Beach Boys Love You*, or a simple rehash of oldies, as was *15 Big Ones*, but, rather, a fully produced spectacle. The songs were melodic ala "Wouldn't It Be Nice" or "Darlin' " and were still contemporary in sound. It was obvious that something had happened between their much - publicized spat and the recording of this album.

"What happened," explains Mike, "is that everyone is working together again. This album, *Winds Of Change*, is showing the collective integration of the band. It wasn't easy.

"This album is the best produced album we've done

since *Pet Sounds*. It really is and I know this album will be a big one for us. *15 Big Ones* was just a bunch of oldies and *Love You* was never finished; Brian was into writing all of these songs and not into producing them.

"What happened to The Beach Boys was that Brian lost his sense of discipline years ago. He was so motivated up until our *Smile* album and then drugs and stuff screwed him up; he lost his sense of competition. For a long time Carl tried to supplement everything and be the leader."

The saga of Brian Wilson has been told several times — and often distorted. However, through meditation at M.I.U. in Santa Barbara (a privately owned center for meditators), Brian Wilson has progressed more in the past eight months than he had in the past eight years.

Mike explains: "What happened was that Brian and I went to MIU and wrote for two weeks. We wrote every day. This was in late September and right after that Alan came out. Ron Altbach, Charles Lloyd and I were all there doing our Celebration thing. We were all there at MIU and lived there for the next three months. We wrote a lot and started the basic tracks for several songs there. We did the bulk of that album and other songs in that three month period. All of The Beach Boys stayed at MIU and we did little weekend dates and college things, but mostly *Winds Of Change* reflects the integration of elements that hasn't been achieved on many Beach Boys' albums because it has always been distracted. It's always been diffused because Brian was into his thing and I was living somewhere else doing mine and everyone was into something else. We all live in different parts of California.

"This time we made a conscious effort and had determination.

"First of all, at MIU the atmosphere is right because everyone is meditating. And there is a facility there available to us that we could use. We did a quick conversion of this hall into a recording studio and we shipped our equipment out there. It was similar to the Holland experiment, but it was more together because we all lived in the same building the whole time."

Chris Walter/RETNA

At MIU, The Beach Boys became a band again. Rather than just grind out another lp at their Brother Studio (which is next to a Sears store in Santa Monica), they decided to experiment with communal living for the duration of the album. It worked.

"Everything worked," Mike boasts. "See, if we needed a vocal, it was right there and if we needed someone to do this number, they were right in the same building. There was a lounge and a dining room and four living quarters, one of which we turned into the studio. The one above the studio was for the staff. There was one for instruments and musicians and one for the Beach Boys themselves. Various suites were made out of these small dormitory rooms. We cut doors between rooms and it took us a month to get the facility ready before we actually moved out there. But I think the album reflects the secludedness of the atmosphere there and the closeness of and the community of us as a group working together as efficiently as we can work together."

Winds Of Change, as it turned out, was the last studio album that The Beach Boys owed Warner Brothers Records. They have already cut some basic tracks for their first Columbia album. The tracks are being cut at Mike Love's property in Santa Barbara (near MIU, but not on the same property).

"I have 11 structures at my place and we'll be doing the next Beach Boys album there. We have been working with

Richard Young/RETNA

Celebration out there and I have some other plans too. I like the cohesiveness of having the production facility and the living space right there. Otherwise it's too distracting to everybody. We all have our own families and we do our own thing here and there. You have to sacrifice these other things to pool your talents together for a time. It doesn't have to be a month at a time either; it could be a week at a time or even a few days at a crack.

"Well, ... at least *Winds Of Change* reflects the collective integration of the band and the atmosphere at MIU. On this album the person who spent the least amount of time there was Dennis. Dennis is really hyper and he was mostly interested in getting back to L.A. and working on his third solo album. He's just doing his own thing, ya know. Dennis does sing lead on 'Diane,' which is a really great song. Brian and I sing lead on a lot of the songs and Alan and Carl are there too; it worked out pretty evenly," says a pleased Mike Love.

The Beach Boys do the Buddy Holly classic "Peggy Sue" on *Winds Of Change*. That is the only oldie of the album though. "Matchpoint Of Our Love" is really the showpiece of the album though; it's a catchy, disco-like tune about sports and love. "Come Go With Me" is another excellent number that brings back the mid-60's Beach Boys sound without sounding dated. There's even a surprise song about surfing in Hawaii and going to a disco

alone. For the first time in almost eight years, I can honestly say that The Beach Boys aren't coasting; they're climbing.

I asked Mike Love if Transcendental Meditation was the reason this album was so strong and positive. I knew the band had always been into TM, but that was something they discovered 10 years ago. Why all of a sudden should it make such a difference?

"I know that TM had everything to do with *Winds Of Change* being a success. All of the guys hadn't been meditating regularly. The influence of MIU and everybody meditating and being regular and going to courses is incredible. A couple of nights a week we'd have a lecture, videotapes and stuff like that, so it was quite a total experience," says Mike.

So, contrary to all of the rumors you've heard about the Beach Boys finally wiping

Aaron/Morley

out, they have never been closer. A band doesn't sign a custom label deal with CBS Records if they are planning on breaking up. The Beach Boys are touring all summer and will have another studio album out before Christmas. Also, expect a solo Mike Love album, a second Dennis Wilson album and a Carl Wilson solo album before the year is out. Also, the third Dennis Wilson album has already been completed and Celebration's first real (not counting the ALMOST SUMMER soundtrack) studio album is being recorded and should be out before 1979 gets too far along.

Could it be true that life begins after 30? □

✱ BRIAN WILSON Tells Why

By now the Beach Boys' story is familiar -- how three brothers, a cousin and a friend became, with their first record over four years ago, America's most popular group. They have spread the "West Coast" sound across their own country and around the world. But what sort of people are the Beach Boys off-stage, out of the short-sleeved, striped shirts, behind the carefree, clean-cut image implicit in their name?

What are these eminently successful and quite rich young men really like to one who knows them well?

There is no one who knows the inside story of the Beach Boys better than Brian Wilson himself, the big brain of the group, who has never written and produced a record flop.

I found the brilliant, thoughtful boy in a reflective mood recently, and what resulted is the following character analysis -- perceptive descriptions of all the other members of the group (and revealing, incidentally, a good deal about his own personality), all in Brian's own words.

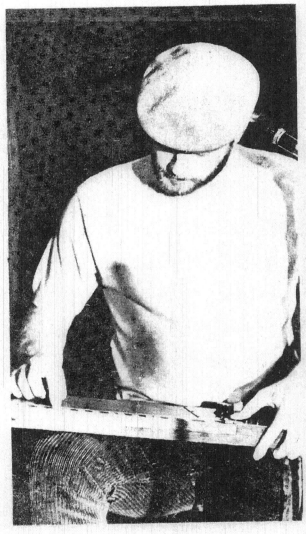

"Mike is the most completely extroverted person I've ever known. He's a great emcee. Al has the greatest most sincere smile in the world. Dennis is the most messed up person I know. He's too nervous. Carl is completely at peace with himself and the world. Bruce is very bouncy and hams it up. Mike has a dry humor and Bruce's is wet. The guys really like him."

He Likes The BEACH BOYS

Mike Love, lead singer. "Mike is the most completely extroverted person I've ever known. It's absolutely fantastic. It will keep him from being very creative.

"To be creative you have to think about things and ways to express them. Mike's too busy being involved in human relationships to sit down and consider them and put them into music.

"He couldn't stand being alone long enough to write something.

"He's a great emcee--very underestimated in that field. In fact, I think he's pretty generally underestimated, but the day will come when *everyone* will appreciate him."

Carl Wilson, lead guitar. "Wow, I can hardly express the great admiration I have for Carl. He's the most truly religious person I know. He's completely at peace with himself and the world and he radiates this.

"People say he's the one who keeps the group from going at each other's throats. It's true -- he can spot a rough situation and avert it before you knew it was there.

"It makes me rather unhappy that I'm only realizing his worth now. You know how teenage boys treat kid brothers. But now, after all those rough years I discover how much we have in common and how much I respect him.

"He's also our best musician. He's starting to write songs and they sound good -- he's still young and I think he'll really expand as he grows older."

Al Jardine, rhythm guitar. "The thing I always think of about Al is that he has the greatest, the most sincere smile in the world. Especially in this business, and in Hollywood, with all the starlets, you see the phoniest smiles.

"But when Al grins, you know it's there! He keeps his opinions to himself all the time. Not because they're not good, but you see, he's not a member of the corporation. *(The Wilson brothers and cousin Mike set up a corporation years ago which handles the group's monetary affairs, etc.)*

"It makes him feel left out and not really at full member of the group, so he doesn't want to force himself or his opinions on us.

"But this feeling is only on his side. As far as the rest of us are concerned, he's got as much right as anyone to give an opinion.

"I wish we could convince him, but no matter what we say, he's always the same. That's just the way Al is -- he's never pushy.

"He's the least wild of the group because he's been married a long time, but he's a bit noisier than Carl. What a smile, though!"

Dennis Wilson, drummer. "Dennis -- oh dear! The most messed up person I know. He's too nervous. He has to keep moving all the time. If you want him to sit still for one second, he's yelling and screaming and ranting and raving.

"I really worry about him. He's going to drive himself -- or everyone else -- crazy. The girls love him, go crazy over him -- he loves it. He's legitimately girl-crazy.

"I think he'd fall apart if they stopped screaming for him. But he drives himself so hard. He loves all kinds of sports. He can't keep quiet or immobile for a second.

"It's like everyone else is on 33½ rpm and he's on 78. I only hope he'll grow out of it as he gets older. I pray for Dennis a lot."

Bruce Johnson, bass guitar. The "6th" Beach Boy who now records with them and takes Brian's former place at all concerts. "I'm afraid I only know Bruce superficially. Of course, I've never been on tour with him or performed with him.

"He's a friend of Mike, who suggested him as my re-

{Continued on next page}

{Continued from last page}

placement. The guys really like him. I only see him at recording sessions.

"He's very bouncy, effervescent. Hams it up a lot. Where Mike has a dry humour, Bruce's is wet!

"I mean, you can tell when he's going to do something funny. But he's very even tempered, which is a good thing when you're recording.

"I think he might have a slight inferiority complex -- nobody's really that bouncy and energetic. He's a very likeable person.

"I'd say Dennis is the hardest to get along with, then Mike, me, Al and Carl. Bruce is down at the bottom, too. It's surprising how long it took for us to have some real understanding of what each other is really like.

"But months of being together forced us to make the effort or we would have broken up.

"You have to learn to understand and accept each other, and to get along with each other if you're traveling and performing and recording together ten months out of the year.

"I'm glad we came out sane and happy." □

By now, Beach Boys' marriages are well known, but we'll tell on them too. Brian married his girlfriend Marilyn. Dennis married Carol who had a 4-year-old son by a previous marriage. Mike married Suzanna after a 6-week courtship. Carl is married to Annie, the sister of Billy Hinsche (Dino, Desi and Billy). Unattached Bruce Johnston poses with his mom. Al Jardine's wife is Linda.

BEACH BOYS: perfect for our Bee Gee age?

How can grown men sing stuff like this and mean it?

BEACH BOYS
'MIU'
(WEA MSK 2268)★★★

THE BEACH Boys never grow up. They seem to be a Peter Pan group, with a direct line to some artesian well of youth, not to say sub-adolescence. And I suffer from a sneaking suspicion that while listening to the new Beach Boys album, my body clock performs a somersault, and I'm 12 again (that means 14 years ago, gee whiz) bopping to the Beach Boys at every party. If there weren't some weirdo psychological reason, how could I get so involved with lyrics that one part of my mind is consciously stating- this is moronic drivel?

'Hey little, hey little, hey little tomboy, it's time you turned into a girl... hmmm, I smell perfume, let's try some cut-off jeans, look at all the changes I see...' ('Hey Little Tomboy' by Brian Wilson).

The first time I heard that lyric, I was aghast. I was even more aghast when I found myself singing along to the limpid harmonies.

As if to assert the primal qualities on this album, the following song, by Al Jardine and Mike Love, is another bug-eyed innocent, a gawpingly romantic Hawaiian travelogue called 'Konna Coast' which burbles 'Waikiki' where 'Barbara Ann' used to be, then glides into a party-down version of Buddy Holly's 'Peggy Sue' which actually quotes 'Barbara Ann' near the end.

In Brian Wilson's absence, the Beach Boys changed into something else entirely — the drifting, languorous explorations of 'Surf's Up' and 'Holland' were a seductive and satisfying maturing process that absorbed me totally. Brian came back, and the band trod water with '15 Big Ones', their excellent tribute/retrospective on influences work. Then it was 'Love You', and back to that

mystifying gawky charm. How could *grown men* be singing this delightful kid's stuff and mean it?

But it was magic, and I played it non-stop, even if it seemed a baffling second adolescence.

And so, here we are, 18 months on and not a day wiser. The Beach Boys have a sweet 'Sunday Love' where they read the funnies in a Sunday morning idyll, drift together past the Seine, feed the pigeons by the Eiffel Tower in 'Belles Of Paris', another incandescent honeymoon travelogue with the harmonies chiming as the bells of Notre Dame, unutterably soppy and so quintessentially romantic it almost hurts to hear it in '78 ('Is this a dream or is it real?' as Tapper Zukie would say).

'Belles Of Paris' is followed by my favourite track 'Pitter Patter', a whole-hearted energising song about how cosy it is to listen to the rain pitter-patter in a room with the one you love, just as slight as it sounds, but an ecstatic paean that exhilarates with every drop drum beat and sudden surge of vocal harmony tinged by the occasional minor surprise twist. I don't know why I love it, but I want to dance round the room

whenever it starts.

They get almost serious next, with Brian Wilson intoning a song to his wife Diane (of American Spring fame) in his new, forced voice, the only sign of the Beach Boys' acne having cleared up. 'Now that you are free, everything is wrong and nothing is right, I want you back with all of my might.' the harmonies soar into fervent counterpoint with the sweeping strings as the band sobs 'I love you, Diane — I'll miss you, Diane' (I didn't even know they'd broken up...)

The album closes on 'Winds Of Change', a sombre, poignant outro with funereal militant drum tattoo, echoing on the words 'Won't last forever'. The symbolism is obvious — the Beach Boys' current delirious nostalgia with its intense harmonies could prove to be perfect for our Bee Gee age, although it sounds drastically irrelevant to contemporary British reality and music. Wait and see, obviously.

Will the world consent to dream of bygone days with the Beach Boys, or are they actually dealing with eternal realities that the Eighties will respond to as ardently as I do?
VIVIEN GOLDMAN

FOUR GIRLS FOR EVERY BOY

SYLVIE SIMMONS shakes the sand out of her tape recorder and aims it at THE BEACH BOYS

PIX BY BRAD ELTERMAN

CALIFORNIA GIRLS: chubby Brian Wilson leching with the cheerleaders at USC.

Leowalski, Ed Cate, Welles Kelly and Gary Griffin, collectively his new band of transcendental meditation practitioners and very, very prolific.

Right now, as well as working on the Beach Boys stuff and their own soundtrack to a forthcoming

---

IMPORTANT DATES in the history of surfing music:

1961 — Formation of the Beach Boys.

1963 — Jan and Dean have a hit with 'Surf City'.

1965 — Brian Wilson has a nervous breakdown and ceases touring with his band.

1966 — Jan Berry is paralysed and near to death from a motor accident.

1973 — An attempt at a revival of Jan and Dean fails horribly.

1975 — The beginning of an attempt by the Beach Boys' record company to flood the market with compilation oldies albums (very successful in U.S.).

1977 — Surf's out and skateboards are in. Skateboarder and teen idol Leif Garrett has the girls with the bushy blonde hairdos running out to buy his hit version of 'Surfin USA'. There's rumours of a Beach Boys split, a final showdown between Mike Love and Dennis Wilson with both off into individual projects.

1978 — Surf's up again. Three albums by the Beach Boys or its members are due on the market by summer', two soundtracks for summer-release films, and tours by the Beach Boys as themselves and as Celebration. You can't miss them. Jan

---

teen-idol cowboy Tim Matheson, due for release in summer), Brian Wilson wrote the music for it and I collaborated on the single which is called 'Almost Summer'. It's a hit album, a hit single and a hit movie. We're promoting it with free concerts at baseball parks, beaches, universities and in street parties around the world. We've been getting requests to come to England and the continent — so I think we will this summer."

Is Celebration going to be a permanent outfit?

"Yes, I think so, because it's a permanent relationship, notably between myself and Ron Altbach and Charles Lloyd, who have common areas of interest and experience in the TM

---

albums, and our own group efforts are what we call Celebration. We're celebrating the positive aspects of life and music."

(Carl Wilson's turn) What part do you play in all this?

"Just a buddy. That's about it."

What else are you up to?

"I'm going up to Santa Barbara (where Mike Love has his seaside home) and we're going to be recording. It's the last album for Warner Brothers." (The Beach Boys owe their old record company one before making a start on their side of their deal with CBS — an astronomical **$8,000,000** contract). "I think it's due for almost immediate release. Then we're working on a new CBS album, which should be ready for late summer release. There's some really strong material on our new album — some real good songs. The last one was okay, it had some nice tunes on it, but we didn't do enough backgrounds or something.

---

boys as themselves and as Celebration. You can't miss them. Jan and Dean are performing individually again, and might make another attempt at a reunion later this year. Surf has resurfaced with a vengeance.

FIRST saw the Beach Boys ten years ago from the front row of the Rainbow (then the Finsbury Park Astoria). They wore Hawaiian shirts, had perfect teeth, and I fell in love with Dennis Wilson. And California. A bunch of us would play Beach Boys records on an old sand-logged portable record player at the beach and dream of palm trees and T-birds and blond bronzed boys who didn't have spots. And sunshine.

It was raining when the Beach Boys played the Los Angeles Forum last December. It was hard to see the band. The kids were more interested in Kiss and skateboards, bad skin problems from all those milkshakes, and the white teeth were hidden behind an intricate scaffolding of braces. There were rumours of a split, a Last Surf. Dreams are easily broken.

Recent reports have shown Dennis, always the black sheep of the family, in custody for corrupting an All-American adolescent girl with this year's hip drug, alcohol. Mike Love has been off attempting to levitate and writing movie scripts with himself in the starring role. He's also been spending a great deal of time with Celebration, saxophonist Charles Lloyd (who played with the Beach Boys on their last tour) and other noted musicians Ron Altbach, Dave Robinson, Mike

working on the Beach Boys stuff and their own soundtrack to a forthcoming summertime movie about drag racing. Celebration are doing a series of free concerts around the States, possibly around the world. And in California at least, Mike and Co have been joined onstage throughout by a happily-performing Brian Wilson (at the Forum concert he did little more than scratch his head and look uncomfortable — here he grabbed a guitar, a tambourine, the piano, anything that made a noise), Carl Wilson, and veteran surfers Jan and Dean.

"The shows — celebrations, parties, a gig by any other name — are all informal, all outdoors. A flashback to a British BB fan's dream. Mike Love framed by palm trees, Carl Wilson silhouetted against sunshine and blue sky. The first freebie is at a small university campus in downtown LA. They've blocked off the street and people are dancing in it. Blond boys in sweat suits, shorts, no shirts, straight from the beaches of your fantasies. For the men there are the young Californian girls of the songs. Blonde and blue-eyed soda-pop cheerleaders sipping Pepsi outside the sorority house and singing the words to all the songs. They're looking out of windows, dancing on the roofs, climbing the palm trees for a better view.

Wolfman Jack climbs out from among a herd of giggling girls and announces the band. Beautiful music. Oldies, plenty of them - 'Good Vibrations', 'Fun Fun Fun', '409', 'I Get Around', 'Surfin USA'. New ones that sound like oldies — 'Almost Summer' and the hauntingly pubescent 'It's Gonna Be A Sad, Sad Summer' (sounds like 'Sealed With A Kiss'). A couple dedicated to our

JAN BERRY and Dean Torrence at USC.

sponsor The Maharishi — 'Song Of Creation' and 'Everyone's In Love With You' — without whom, I discover, none of this would have been possible. Classics, 'Summer In The City' and 'Dancing In The Moonlight'. A Beach Boys show plus. Dean Torrence, and then his old partner, Jan Berry, come onto the makeshift stage for poignant if painful-on-the-ears versions of 'Surf City' and 'Little Old Lady From Pasadena'. — 'It sounded all right last night in the garage,' sang an off-key Dean. California girls sing 'California Girls' and the boys sound like they mean it.

DEAN TORRENCE, Brian Wilson, Mike Love and Carl Wilson on stage.

Everyone's dancing, everyone's smiling. Old dreams never really die.

A Few Words From Our Leader
(Mike Love apparently believes this is a radio interview.)

"Hi. I'm Mike Love here at USC and this is the Almost Summer Celebration you're witnessing. It's the first actual event Celebration are playing. The idea is it's almost summer, there's a movie called 'Almost Summer' (starring Didi Conn of 'You Light Up My Life' infamy, Dennis Wilson's old lady Karen Lamm, and

program, and (plug) its benefits not only to ourselves but hopefully to the world at large. We just spent six months together at an advanced course on the TM Siddhi program, as it's called, experimenting and experiencing higher states of consciousness. Celebration is the musical vehicle of expression to the surplus of creativity and energy that we gained from our involvement in the transcendental meditation program. I wrote about 50 songs in a couple of months at that course, and we just needed an outlet. So we're doing soundtracks, we're doing individual

but we didn't do enough backgrounds or something. We'll be touring, doing a few dates this month including A Day On The Green (a San Franciscan festival). We hit the road properly in June.

'Today we were talking with our management about doing a festival in England and a few more dates in London and Europe. There are a lot of things going on.' (A spokesman claimed that the band would more likely be doing just one date in Britain, a summer festival probably, and one concert in each European country).

What about the bad press — the split, Dennis's latest escapade, problems with alcohol?

"It's all very sensational, but that's the way it goes. We had a scene last year — it really was a scene. It really came to a deal there in the airport in New York (where the band members took off in separate planes, reportedly).

CONTINUED ON P. 41

BEACH BOYS

from page 21

vowing never to darken each others' doors again). It's all over.''

A word from surfer boy Dean Torrence, who is hanging out by the girls dorm.

"I'm standing here in this sorority house in Southern California, and it's as close as I've been to Paradise in a while. There's a room up there with an extra bed and there's about five or six girls in that room (two girls for every boy?) and I'm just kind of floating. I'm more excited than I've been in a long time. I'm going to Santa Barbara tomorrow with Celebration. This is like a test thing for me to see if it sounds all right for all of us. Mike and I have always wanted to work together, and this is the first opportunity we've had to see if it works. I might join the band if it happens today.''

How do you feel about TM?
"I don't know about that yet. I get, I think, two more lectures and then I get initiated. I'm looking forward to it. Maybe it'll work, maybe it won't, but it's not going to hurt to try. $160 — that's the only thing that's bothering me. But I'll borrow it from my mom or somebody.''

Does Jan Berry's appearance on stage with you herald a Jan and Dean reunion?
"This is my first time with the band, so I don't know when we'll be working Jan in right now; but we are doing some old Jan and Dean material. There's been a renewed interest in Jan & Dean because of the movie, which will probably be released in Europe this summer.
"I'm thinking maybe we'll pick out four or five major cities in the US and do a Jan & Dean Thankyou America concert. It's been so long since we've been on stage together, and to have our own thing just wouldn't be as polished. But if we were part of somebody else's show, like Celebration — just plugged in and unplugged out again — I think it could work out real nice. Jan has his own band ("It's called The Rock and Roll Band and there are four men — lead guitar, bass, keyboard and drums,'' says Berry. "They live in Pueblo Colorado and they're going to tour all around the nation on May 15th. They're really wild. I've got my thing together a little bit, and it's a nice spirit.'').
"He's playing a lot of clubs — I hate to play clubs, but if he doesn't mind, it's up to him. His band is basically a pick-up band he's put together in the last two or three months, people coming in and out. I'd rather do this.''

Is this a Surf Revival?
"Well, we're the first generation surfers, and the second generation. Maybe even the third. It's going to be an interesting evolution anyway; and it's going to go on.''
What you might call permanent wave. The boys in the band go off into the back room to jam together. When you catch a wave you're sitting on top of the world.

BRIAN WILSON, Mike Love and Carl Wilson plus a bunch of busty California girls.

SURF'S UP!
Brian Wilson Comes Back From Lunch

by Richard Cromelin

[The following was gleaned from two conversations with Brian Wilson. His publicist had warned: "You don't just sit down and interview Brian. He'll talk for ten minutes and then be gone." Au contraire, we found that Brian spoke candidly and at length, until—without warning—he ended the sessions with an abrupt "That should about wrap it."

The first talk was over lunch at a Beverly Hills restaurant. Attending were Brian, his wife Marilyn, his press agent, his psychiatrist, and his psychiatrist's assistant, who described Brian's current therapy: "He's learning how to develop a style of being able to take care of himself, to feel accepting, feel OK about who he is and what he can create." We don't know about that; sounds suspiciously like the ubiquitous est—TM, sorry—that's fueling the BB's now, in place of milkshakes and surf's up and sunny Cal-i-forn-i-ay. At any rate, Brian, a hulking behemoth of a man (though he's slimmed down somewhat) arranged a second meeting at his house, and although going over the traumas of the past seemed to cause him pain, once he got going on the present he relaxed and started to enjoy himself. Without his psychiatrist present. Read on—Ed.]

* * *

CREEM: Why did you finally return to the studio on *15 Big Ones*?

BRIAN: Well, we did it for two reasons. One, the natural spring cycle had arrived and we felt creative this time. Two, we had an obligation to Warner Brothers to make the delivery of the album, and we hadn't really been fulfilling our commitment, so we had to get with it and get the stuff done.

CREEM: Why had it been so long since you worked?

> **I was hiding in my bedroom from the world. I was unhealthy, I was way overweight, I was totally a vegetable. It happened through my starting to take drugs.**

BRIAN: I was hiding in my bedroom from the world. Basically, I had been just out of commission. I was unhealthy, I was way overweight, I was totally a vegetable. In other words, my life got all screwed up. It happened through my starting to take drugs. I started taking a lot of cocaine and a lot of drugs, and it threw me inward—I imploded. I withdrew from society and continued to do so for about four years, until January or February of this year.

My wife had a psychiatrist, Dr. Gene Landy, commissioned to straighten me up. It took a couple of months, but they did it, through enforcement of no drugs, bodyguards at my house, working, a physical education program and so on.

CREEM: You were just sitting in your room?

BRIAN: Yeah, I was meditating. I took up meditation a couple of years ago, and that turned me inward too.

Dave Patrick

Dennis go sleep. I go bye-bye. Hu-hut!

CREEM: There was a mystique that grew around you in the Sixties when you were working on *Pet Sounds* and *Smile* about being reclusive and all that. How did you relate to that mystique?

BRIAN: Well, I got behind that, because it's all true. I was a hermit. I was a musical hermit and I did stay alone. It's true that I did have a sandbox in my house. It was the size of one room and we had a piano in the sand. The story about staying home and writing in the sandbox is all true, and it's pretty close to how I really am.

The mystique grew, and I was getting fascinated with the fact that I was becoming famous and that there was interest in my style of life. I had a certain style of life, you know, a very eccentric person, and people began making note of that.

CREEM: Why did you stop touring with the Beach Boys?

BRIAN: Well, I had a nervous breakdown at the end of 1964.

CREEM: Is touring what led up to the nervous breakdown?

BRIAN: Yes, it really was . . . The grueling touring life; that's a strain on the nervous system. The worst part of it was the loud sounds that came out on stage. See, I have only one ear that works, so I have twice as much sound going in one ear, and all that sound drove me nuts, drove me to a nervous breakdown.

I just remember that I started to flip out-and I slammed the door on Carl [Wilson] and said 'Get out of here. I don't want to see anybody.' I told an airline stewardess that I didn't want any food, to get away from me, things like that, I was crying on the plane and everything. That was the start of the secluded period, which ended with "California Girls."

Then I had another nervous breakdown in 1972, after we went to Holland. I'd been away from home too long. See, my wife pulled our studio out of my house in '72, so in June of '72 we all hauled off to Holland and built a studio, did some recording and ended up staying five and a half

> "The Beach Boys were going through a rebellious period, and they were actually denying the songs that made them famous."

months. Well, as a combination of things that happened over there, plus being away from home, I had a little breakdown over there. I couldn't take the idea of being away from home that long. I'm almost a Cancer, I'm June 20th, so I have a little Cancer in me, which is very devoted to home and wanting to stay there. The security is the home—California and this place.

CREEM: I've read that you don't relate to the California mystique anymore.

BRIAN: We summed up our desire to get back to that feeling in "Do It Again." It's not just surfing; it's the outdoors and cars and sunshine; it's the society of California; it's the way of California . . . I don't feel that's past, no. We're fools to neglect that aspect. I relate to it more than I did because I'm more aware of the beauties of that type of social concept. Those types of records, those types of ideas; I mean they're gold, they're sheer gold, and those are the kinds of things the Beach Boys should stick with.

CREEM: There was a point where the group seemed to be rejecting the surf songs.

BRIAN: They were denying that whole success period. They were going through a rebellious period, and they were actually denying the songs that made them famous, but then they got back into what I call being proud of one's thing, and I think it's working better for them now. They got very arty and they thought maybe they didn't have to carry that with them. But any artist should know that you carry along that which made you famous when you do your show.

CREEM: How did it feel to be back in the studio again?

BRIAN: Well, it was a little scary, because we weren't as close. We drifted apart personality wise. A lot of guys had developed new personalities through meditation. There had been so many changes in our personalities that our getting back together was a bit scary and shaky. But we socked into that studio with the attitude that we had to get it done, so we worked out of necessity.

After a week or two of being in the studio we started to get into the niche again. But it took a while, because we hadn't been together in the studio in those conditions in so long.

CREEM: Are your days of experimentation in the studio over?

BRIAN: No. We have some ambitions. We're thinking about that right now . . . I want to try to get into that in the future, to make another *Smile*.

CREEM: But the *Smile* album never came out. What happened?

BRIAN: Well, we got a little arty about it, and it got to the point where we were too selfishly artistic and we weren't thinking about the public enough. It got to that level. Partially because of drugs . . .

CREEM: Was there ever a point when you were taking drugs that you felt it was beneficial?

BRIAN: Yes, several years ago, back when I was working with Van Dyke Parks, he and I both took drugs to work

TURN TO PAGE 76

193

BRIAN WILSON

CONTINUED FROM PAGE 30.

together and it worked to the positive.

CREEM: What was the reaction of the rest of the group to the stuff you were doing for *Smile* and *Pet Sounds*?

BRIAN: I think they thought that it was for Brian Wilson only. They knew that Brian Wilson was gonna be a separate entity, something that was a force of his own, and it was generally considered that the Beach Boys were the main thing. So with *Pet Sounds* there was a resistance in that I was doing most of the artistic work on it vocally, and for that reason there was a little bit of intergroup struggle. It was resolved in the fact that they figured that it was a showcase for Brian Wilson, but it's still the Beach Boys. In other words, they gave in. They let me have my little stint.

CREEM: How did you feel about *Pet Sounds* being hailed as a masterpiece, the first concept album?

BRIAN: Well, I felt that the production was a masterpiece. *Pet Sounds* was an offshoot of the Phil Spector production technique. I'm proud of it for that reason, in that we were able to produce tracks that had a monumental sound to them. It had that wall of sound touch to it. My contribution was adding the harmonies, learning to incorporate harmonies and certain vocal techniques to that Spector production concept that I learned.

But *Pet Sounds* wasn't really conceived as a "concept album." It was a production concept album. It wasn't really a song concept album or lyrically a concept album.

CREEM: What do you think your other important contributions have been?

BRIAN: I think that "Good Vibrations" was a contribution in that it was a pocket symphony, it had a pocket symphony effect . . . It was a series of intricate harmonies and mood changes. We used a cello for the first time in rock 'n' roll, so I think in that respect it was an innovation . . .

"Good Vibrations" . . . an adult could even say, 'Yeah, now there is a deep thought!' I think "Good Vibrations" is the most adult masterpiece we've ever done and I'm very proud of it.

CREEM: How did "Good Vibrations" come about?

BRIAN: My mother used to talk about vibrations when I was a kid . . . She told me that dogs pick up vibrations, and they bark at some people and don't bark at others. She said that people pick up vibrations too. Then some years later, I came up with a song which was about that very concept, about people picking up vibrations from other people.

CREEM: What did you think of Todd Rundgren's version of "Good Vibrations" on *Faithful*?

BRIAN: Oh, he did a marvelous job, he did a great job. I was very proud of his version.

CREEM: Are you still interested in progressive records?

BRIAN: I am, but I haven't found as many as I used to find, though now and then you will find. for instance, Queen. They made a record called "Bohemian Rhapsody" which to me was a fulfillment of artistic music. I studied the record, I became very familiar with it, and I'm very, very fond of it and scared of it at the same time.

CREEM: Why, because of the competitive thing?

BRIAN: Oh, it's the most competitive thing that's come along in ages. It's just totally amazing what people do when they lose their noggins, when they lose their heads and go in there and freak. That's exactly what Queen did. They had enough of what was happening, and by God, they went in and did their thing and stomped. And I appreciate that and I'm very fond of it.

I think records have now gotten to the point where now everything is its own identity. There are not very many fads nowadays that you can really follow. Especially in production. I think the great era of production is over.

CREEM: Could you talk about the contribution or role of each person in the group?

BRIAN: I see Mike Love as one of the best lead singers in that he sounds young . . . He's in tune with the teenagers, with the 16 to 25 age group. Dennis Wilson maintains a steady image of his own kind of singing. I would consider him hitting the 25 to 35 age bracket. Al Jardine is also like Mike Love; he sounds young. So Al and Mike are responsible for our youth, Carl Wilson and Dennis are responsible for 25 to 45 and I think I'm responsible for 25 to 45. So it's a careful blending of age groups that we hit.

CREEM: Do you think like that a lot, in terms of age groups?

BRIAN: Yeah, I do, because I think that music has become stereotyped and it's been bagged. I think that if you spread your music around, you'll take in an older audience. But I think you have to be constantly aware of the teenagers. We still should be making music for the kids. I see no reason to desert that audience.

CREEM: That audience deserted you for a while, right?

BRIAN: Yes, they did. They deserted us. We made records that just didn't make it.

CREEM: Why have the Beach Boys remained together as long as they have?

BRIAN: Because we're a family, and the family that sings together stays together. That's been proved by the Beach Boys a hundred times over. That's the overwhelming reason we've had our success and why we've stayed together.

The other minor reason was me. my love for music and my competitiveness. I was a "better, better, better" type, what's that called? . . . One-upsmanship, yeah. I was glued to that aspect. I thought that was the way. And that *is* the way. You should never think that what you did before is gonna be as good as what you're doing now.

Printed in Great Britain
by Amazon.co.uk, Ltd.,
Marston Gate.